Margaret von Ziegésar / Detlef von Ziegésar

Training Intensiv

Grammatik

Englisch

Klett Lerntraining

Illustrationen:
Andreas Florian, Lübeck: Seiten 12, 21, 22, 78, 161;
Hitz und Mahn, Stuttgart: Seiten 34, 36, 37, 54, 56, 78, 102, 112, 138;
Ingo Schimazek, Rheinstetten: Seiten 57, 65, 94

Abbildungsverzeichnis:
Cartoon von Express Newspapers 1983: Seite 41;
Cartoon von The Mirror, 21.9.1985: Seite 81;
Cartoon von The Mirror, 15.6.1985: Seite 101;
Cartoons aus: D. and R. Manley: The Piccolo Book of Cartoons, Pan 1977: Seiten 31, 53, 65, 90, 91, 95, 123, 138

Bibliographische Information der Deutschen Bibliothek
Die Deutsche Bibliothek verzeichnet diese Publikation in der Deutschen Nationalbibliografie; detaillierte bibliografische Daten sind im Internet über http://dnb.ddb.de abrufbar.

Auflage 4. 3. 2. | 2013 2012
Die letzten Zahlen bezeichnen jeweils die Auflage und das Jahr des Druckes.
Dieses Werk folgt der reformierten Rechtschreibung und Zeichensetzung.
Das Werk und seine Teile sind urheberrechtlich geschützt. Jede Nutzung in anderen als den gesetzlich zugelassenen Fällen bedarf der vorherigen schriftlichen Einwilligung des Verlages. Hinweis zu § 52a UrhG: Weder das Werk noch seine Teile dürfen ohne eine solche Einwilligung eingescannt und in ein Netzwerk eingestellt werden. Dies gilt auch für Intranets von Schulen und sonstigen Bildungseinrichtungen.
Fotomechanische Wiedergabe nur mit Genehmigung des Verlages.
© Klett Lerntraining GmbH, Stuttgart 2010
Alle Rechte vorbehalten.
Internetadresse: www.klett.de/lernhilfen
Umschlaggestaltung: Sabine Kaufmann, Stuttgart
Satz: Klaus Bauer, Bondorf
Reproduktion: Meyle + Müller, Medien-Management, Pforzheim
Druck: Medienhaus Plump, Rheinbreitbach
Printed in Germany
ISBN 978-3-12-927216-9

Inhalt

1 Simple present – present progressive 8

Überprüfen Sie Ihr Wissen 9
§ 1 Gebrauch des simple present 10
§ 2 Gebrauch des present progressive 11
Übungen 12
§ 3 Statische Verben, normalerweise im simple present 13
§ 4 Zustandsverben im simple present und im present progressive 14
Übungen 15

2 Simple past – present perfect 16

Überprüfen Sie Ihr Wissen 17
§ 1 Gebrauch des simple past 18
§ 2 Gebrauch des present perfect 18
§ 3 Zeitadverbien im present perfect und im simple past 20
Übungen 21

3 Past progressive – simple past 24

Überprüfen Sie Ihr Wissen 25
§ 1 Gebrauch des past progressive 26
§ 2 Past progressive und simple past im Vergleich 27
Übungen 28

4 Present perfect progressive – present perfect simple – past perfect 32

Überprüfen Sie Ihr Wissen 33
§ 1 Gebrauch des present perfect progressive 34
Übungen 35
§ 2 Present perfect simple und present perfect progressive im Vergleich 36
Übungen 38
§ 3 Present perfect progressive und simple past im Vergleich 40
§ 4 Simple past, present perfect simple und progressive form im Überblick 40
Übungen 41
§ 5 Gebrauch des past perfect 43

5 Future time 44

Überprüfen Sie Ihr Wissen 45
§ 1 Übersicht über die verschiedenen Futurformen 46
§ 2 Das will-future 47

§ 3 Das going to-future 48
Übungen 49
§ 4 Das present progressive-future 50
Übungen 50
§ 5 Das simple present-future 51
Übungen 52
§ 6 Das future progressive 54
Übungen 55
§ 7 Das future perfect simple und progressive 56
Übungen 57

6 Modals 58

Überprüfen Sie Ihr Wissen 59
§ 1 Can – could – could have; can't – can't have – couldn't have; be able to 60
Übungen 62
§ 2 Must – mustn't 64
Übungen 65
§ 3 Must have 67
Übungen 67
§ 4 Have to – not have to 68
Übungen 70
§ 5 Needn't/not have to – mustn't – needn't have – didn't need to 71
Übungen 72
§ 6 May – might – may/might as well 73
Übungen 75
§ 7 Shall/should – should have – be to/be supposed to – ought to – had better 76
Übungen 78
§ 8 Will 79
Übungen 80
§ 9 Want – would 81
Übungen 81

7 Infinitive – ing-form 82

Überprüfen Sie Ihr Wissen 83
§ 1 Der Infinitiv mit to 84
Übungen 86
§ 2 Der Infinitiv ohne to 87
Übungen 88
§ 3 Die ing-Form (gerund) 89
Übungen 90

§ 4 Verben mit Infinitiv und ing-Form 92
Übungen 94

8 Participles 96

Überprüfen Sie Ihr Wissen 98
§ 1 Partizipien anstelle adverbialer Gliedsätze 99
Übungen 101
§ 2 Partizipien nach bestimmten Verben 104
Übungen 104
§ 3 Idiomatische Wendungen mit Partizipien 105
Übungen 105

9 If-clauses 106

Überprüfen Sie Ihr Wissen 107
§ 1 If, when 108
Übungen 108
§ 2 If-Sätze vom Typ A: wahrscheinliche Bedingungen 109
§ 3 Will/should in Bedingungssätzen 110
Übungen 111
§ 4 If-Sätze vom Typ B: irreale Bedingungen 113
Übungen 115
§ 5 If-Sätze vom Typ C: nicht mehr erfüllbare Bedingungen 117
Übungen 118

10 Comparison of adjectives 120

Überprüfen Sie Ihr Wissen 121
§ 1 Die regelmäßigen Steigerungsformen: Komparativ und Superlativ 122
§ 2 Die unregelmäßigen Steigerungsformen: Komparativ und Superlativ 123
Übungen 123
§ 3 Vergleiche mit than, (not) as … as, (bigg)er and (bigg)er, the (soon)er … the bett(er) 124
Übungen 125

11 Adverbs 128

Überprüfen Sie Ihr Wissen 129
§ 1 Arten der Adverbien 130
§ 2 Die Bildung von Adverbien 131
Übungen 133
§ 3 Adverbien der Zeit (adverbs of time) 134

Übungen 136
§ 4 Adverbien des Ortes/der Richtung (adverbs of place) 137
Übungen 138
§ 5 Adverbien der Art und Weise (adverbs of manner) 139
§ 6 Adverbien der Häufigkeit (adverbs of frequency) 140
§ 7 Adverbien des Grades (adverbs of degree) 141
Übungen 142
§ 8 Hervorhebende Adverbien (focusing adverbs) 144
Übungen 144
§ 9 Satzadverbien (sentence adverbs) 145
Übungen 145
§ 10 Inversion 146
Übungen 146
§ 11 Englische Verben anstelle deutscher Adverbien 147
Übungen 147

12 Indirect speech 148

Überprüfen Sie Ihr Wissen 149
§ 1 Die Funktionen der indirekten Rede 150
Übungen 151
§ 2 Einleitendes Verb im present tense, present perfect, future:
   keine Veränderung der direkten Rede 152
Übungen 152
§ 3 Einleitendes Verb im simple past oder past progressive:
   keine Veränderung der direkten Rede 153
Übungen 156
§ 4 Einleitendes Verb im simple past oder past progressive:
   Veränderungen in der direkten Rede 157
Übungen 158
§ 5 Die modalen Hilfsverben in der indirekten Rede,
   einleitendes Verb im past tense 159
Übungen 160
§ 6 Veränderungen bei Pronomina, Zeit- und Ortsangaben, Fragen 162
Übungen 164

Lösungen 165

Vorwort

Training Intensiv „Englische Grammatik" hilft allen, die die englische Grammatik wiederholen und üben möchten.
Der Schwerpunkt liegt auf den grammatischen Strukturen, die häufig Schwierigkeiten machen. Wenn Sie glauben, eine grammatische Struktur nicht sicher zu beherrschen, können Sie hier **nachschlagen**, **wiederholen** und **üben**. Das Buch kann natürlich auch als reines Nachschlagewerk benutzt werden.

So arbeiten Sie mit diesem Buch:

Suchen Sie mit Hilfe des Inhaltsverzeichnisses die grammatischen Gebiete heraus, die Ihnen Schwierigkeiten bereiten. Die grammatischen Gebiete sind in zwölf Kapitel mit jeweils mehreren Paragrafen unterteilt.

Jedes Kapitel beginnt mit einer Übersicht der grammatischen Strukturen. Diese Übersicht gibt Ihnen eine erste Orientierung und reaktiviert bereits vorhandenes Wissen.

Testen Sie nun Ihr Vorwissen in dem Abschnitt „Überprüfen Sie Ihr Wissen". Sie verschaffen sich damit mehr Klarheit darüber, wo Ihre Probleme liegen. Erst wenn Sie alle Test-Aufgaben gelöst haben, vergleichen Sie Ihre Antworten mit denen im Lösungsteil. Im **Lösungsteil** sind alle erwarteten Antworten mit den Nummern der Kapitel und Paragrafen versehen, in denen sie grammatikalisch ausführlich erklärt werden.

Diesen aus Beispielsätzen und Regeln bestehenden Erklärungen **(Wissen)** wenden Sie sich in all jenen Fällen zu, in denen Sie unsicher waren oder Fehler machten.

In einem nächsten Schritt bearbeiten Sie die nachfolgenden **Übungen**. Schließen Sie immer eine Übung ganz ab und vergleichen Sie Ihre Antwort mit den Lösungen.

Zur Systematisierung Ihres Sprachwissens und -könnens lesen Sie abschließend die gesammelten Regeln des von Ihnen jeweils ausgewählten Grammatikparagrafen durch.

Wir wünschen Ihnen viel Erfolg!

1 Simple present – present progressive

In diesem Kapitel wiederholen wir alles, was Sie wissen müssen, um die **simple present**- und **present progressive**-Formen richtig anwenden zu können. Prüfen Sie jetzt bitte nach, ob Sie die beiden Zeitformen richtig benutzen können.

Einige Beispiele für diese zwei Formen:

simple present	present progressive
Ken **works** in a supermarket.	Ken **is working** in York at the moment.
Ann **watches** TV every night.	Ann **is watching** TV.
I **speak** French.	Tony **is learning** Spanish.
Wolfgang **comes** from Germany.	Jill **is staying** with me this week.
The earth **goes** round the sun.	It**'s getting** warmer.
What **happens** in the film?	What**'s happening** outside?
What **do** I **do** next?	You**'re always** listening to music.
It **depends** on the weather.	It**'s raining**.
That CD **belongs** to me.	Sally **is being** silly today.
How much **do** you **weigh**?	I**'m trying** to eat less.
I **think** you're right.	My brother **is thinking** of going to England.

Überprüfen Sie Ihr Wissen

1

Es ist sehr wichtig, dass Sie die zwei Formen richtig anwenden können, denn sie verändern die Bedeutung einer Äußerung. Bemerken Sie z. B., welche unterschiedlichen Bedeutungen diese zwei Sätze haben?

a) Margaret **lives** in Sheffield.

b) Margaret **is living** in Sheffield.

2

Choose the simple present or present progressive forms of the verbs in brackets.

1. Would you like some beer? – No, thanks. I … alcohol. (not drink)
2. Why … you … French? (learn) Because I … to go to France next summer. (want)
3. Where … you … from? (come)
4. What … your father … for a living? (do)
5. My sister … to be a nurse. (train)
6. That's an interesting article. It … you all about British teenagers. (tell)
7. What … you …? (read) A thriller. It's very good.
8. Where … I … a ticket, please? (get)
9. I don't like Mr Smith. He … too much. (talk)
10. Carol, hurry up! What … you … in the bathroom all this time? (do)
11. How … you … these days? (get on)
12. What language … they … in Peru? (speak)
13. I think it … colder. We'd better take coats. (get)
14. I hate my uncle. He …. always … me about girlfriends. (ask)

Im Folgenden wiederholen wir alle Regeln, die Sie brauchen, um die zwei Formen richtig anwenden zu können. In den sich anschließenden Übungen können Sie überprüfen, ob Sie die Regeln verstanden haben.

1 Simple present – present progressive   Wissen

§1 Gebrauch des simple present

Man verwendet das *simple present* für:

§1.1	Ken **works** in a supermarket. Paul **watches** TV every night. Tony **plays** the guitar in a band. past now future	Berufsmäßige und sonstige **gewohnheitsmäßige Tätigkeiten**. Typische Zeitbestimmungen: *every (day), normally, usually, always, never*
§1.2	My brother only **drinks** milk. I **speak** French and German. My mother **enjoys** thrillers.	Typische **Eigenschaften, Fähigkeiten** und **Einstellungen**. Typische Verben: *to love, to enjoy, to hate, to like, to allow, to say*
§1.3	Where **do** you **come** from? I **come** from Germany. The earth **goes** round the sun.	Tatsachen und Dauerzustände, die als **zeitlos gültig** angesehen werden.
§1.4	What **happens** in the film? What **does** Tony **say** in his letter? He **explains** why he can't come to the wedding. The article **deals** with the problems of pollution.	**Inhaltsangaben** (Buch, Film, Brief, Telefongespräch, Zeitungsartikel); **Inhalte erfragen**; Schlagzeilen.
§1.5	… Jones **passes** the ball to Williams. Williams **runs** towards the goal … Now watch: First I **pour** the water into the glass. Then I **add** …	**Begleitkommentar oder Beschreibung** zu einer Aufeinanderfolge von Handlungen, z. B. Sportreportagen, Experimente, Kochrezepte usw.
§1.6	What **do** I **do** next? How **do** we **get** to the station? Let me help you to fill in the form: first you **write** your name at the top.	**Anweisungen und Auskünfte.**
§1.7	I was waiting for the bus this morning. Then a man **comes** up to me and **says** …	Die **lebendigere oder dramatischere Darstellung** vergangener Ereignisse.

§ 2 Gebrauch des present progressive

Man verwendet das *present progressive* für:

§ 2.1	I'm just **doing** my homework. past — now — future	Vorgänge, die **im Moment des Sprechens** ablaufen. Typische Zeitbestimmungen: *just, (just) now, at the moment*
§ 2.2	Sue **is learning** French. I'm **trying** to stop smoking. past — future	Vorgänge, die **begonnen haben und noch nicht zu Ende sind**, die aber auch gerade unterbrochen sein können. Unser Augenmerk ist auf eine bestimmte Zeitspanne gerichtet.
§ 2.3	Jill **is staying** with me at the moment. around now past — now — future	Vorgänge, die **vorübergehender Natur** sind. Typische adverbiale Bestimmungen: *at the moment, these days, this week*
§ 2.4	The weather **is getting** warmer. 14° 18° 20° past — now — future The leaves **are turning** brown.	**Veränderungen** während einer begrenzten Zeitspanne, die die Gegenwart einschließt.
§ 2.5	You're always **listening** to music. (Das geht mir auf die Nerven) **Vergleiche:** You always **listen** to music, don't you? (Du magst wohl gerne Musik?) Jane **is** always **telling** funny stories. (Das finde ich toll) Jane always **tells** funny stories when I go to see her. (Nur zu diesen Zeiten)	**Gefühlsbetonte Beschreibungen** von Gewohnheiten, häufig mit *always*. Der Sprecher drückt Verärgerung, Verwunderung oder Belustigung aus.

1 Simple present – present progressive   Übungen

1
Can you find the right pairs?

1. What are you doing?
2. What do you do for a living?
3. Would you like one?
4. Do you still smoke?
5. When do you have lunch?
6. Will you ring Diane for me?

a) No, thanks. I don't smoke.
b) I'm making a cupboard.
c) Yes, but later. She's just having lunch.
d) From twelve to one.
e) I make furniture.
f) Well, I'm just trying to stop.

2
This is Brenda relaxing at home. Look at the picture and write as much as you can about her. Use as many different verbs as you can.

§ 3 Statische Verben, normalerweise im simple present

Es gibt einige Verben, die im Allgemeinen nur im *simple present* stehen.
Sie drücken nämlich nicht einen Prozess *(present progressive)*, sondern einen
Zustand, eine **Meinung**, **Einstellung** oder **Sinneswahrnehmung** aus.
Hierher gehören:

§ 3.1	My father **is** a teacher. Those trousers **look** nice. The train **seems** to have left. That **sounds** like a fire-engine.	**Zustandsverben:** a) Was jemand ist; der Anschein: *be, look, seem, sound*
	That book **belongs** to me.	b) Was jemand besitzt: *belong, have (got), own*
	I don't know if I'm coming. It **depends on** the weather.	c) Verben, die eine Beziehung ausdrücken: *contain, depend on*
	How much **does** it **cost**? How much **do** you **weigh**?	d) Kosten, Maße: *cost, measure, weigh*
§ 3.2	I **agree** with you. You **believe** me, don't you? Do you **know** what I mean? What **does** this word **mean**?	Verben, die eine **Meinung**, **Vermutung** oder **Wissen** ausdrücken: *agree, believe, forget, know, mean (meinen, bedeuten), remember, suppose, think, understand*
§ 3.3	My cat **hates** dogs. Do you **mind** if I open the window? Who **wants** an ice-cream?	Verben, die eine **gefühlsmäßige Einstellung** ausdrücken: *hate, hope, like, love, mind, need, prefer, want, wish*
§ 3.4	I **hear** you passed your exam. I **notice** you've stopped smoking.	Verben der **Sinneswahrnehmung**: *see, hear, feel, taste, smell, notice*

1 Simple present – present progressive

Wissen

§ 4 Zustandsverben im simple present und im present progressive

Sie haben vielleicht schon bemerkt, dass einige dieser statischen Verben manchmal doch im *present progressive* erscheinen. Wie erklärt sich das? Manche dieser Verben haben eine ganz andere Bedeutung, wenn sie in der *progressive form* erscheinen:

§ 4	simple present	present progressive
be	Sally **is** normally very sensible. (= sein)	Sally **is being** silly today. (= sich benehmen)
have	Brenda **has** two children. (= haben)	Karin **is having** a baby. (= schwanger sein)
see	You can **see** Dover from here. (= sehen)	Mrs Bailey **is** just **seeing** a customer. (= sich unterhalten, sich treffen)
think	I **don't think** you're right. (= glauben)	My brother **is thinking** of going to England next summer. (= planen)

3

Put the verbs in brackets into either the simple present or the present progressive. Do all the sentences before you look at the answers.

1. … you … to go and see a film?
   (want)
2. You … always … me to be quiet.
   (tell)
3. This plant looks as if it … .
   (die)
4. Marie's parents … not … her go to a disco.
   (let)
5. I … you have passed your exam. That's great.
   (hear)
6. Wendy's on the phone. She … she'll be here at seven.
   (say)
7. Andy … like his brother, doesn't he?
   (look)
8. My bike's broken down, so I … by bus this week.
   (travel)
9. What time … your mother usually … home from work?
   (get)
10. What's that noise? – It … like a helicopter.
    (sound)
11. I don't want any chips. I … .
    (slim)
12. My penfriend … from Wales.
    (come)
13. I've just read a fantastic book. It's about a woman who stole some jewelry from a shop.
    First she … to sell it, then she … out that the shop … to the mafia.
    (try, find, belong)
14. I don't know how to play this game. What … I …?
    (do)
    – Watch me. First I … . the cards in front of me. Then I … one from the pile in the middle.
    (put, take)
15. … this dog … to you?
    (belong)

Before you look at the answers write down which rules helped you.

2 Simple past – present perfect

Sie wissen sicher aus Erfahrung, dass die richtige Anwendung des *present perfect* und *simple past* gar nicht so einfach ist. Aber keine Angst! Wenn Sie sich ein paar Regeln merken, ist es nicht so schwer.

Zunächst einige Beispiele für die zwei Formen:

present perfect	simple past
I **have been** at this school for five years.	I **was** at this school for five years.
Susan **has** just **kissed** me.	Susan **kissed** me last night.
Someone **has shot** the bank manager.	Someone **shot** the bank manager yesterday afternoon.
I **haven't had** lunch yet.	We **had** lunch an hour ago.
Have you **heard** the news?	I **heard** about the accident last night.
I **have seen** that film.	I **saw** that film last week.
Have you ever **been** in love?	I **was** in love twice last year.

Prüfen Sie jetzt bitte nach, inwieweit Sie diese zwei Zeitformen richtig anwenden können.

Überprüfen Sie Ihr Wissen

Complete these sentences by putting the words in brackets into either the simple past or the present perfect.

1. Brian … a laptop a few months ago. (buy)
2. I didn't know Brian had a laptop. –
   Yes, he … it for a few months now. (have)
3. Last year we … to Wales for our holidays. (go)
4. You're brown! – Yes, I … on holiday. (just be)
5. I can't come to the football match. I … my homework yet. (not do)
6. I … all my homework yesterday afternoon. (do)
7. Are you tired? – Yes, I … very well last night. (not sleep)
8. Are you tired? – Yes, I … a hard day. (have)
9. Here is the nine o'clock news: There … an accident on the M1 near Nottingham. (be)
10. I … my keys. (lose) … you … them with you this morning? (take)
11. Where … you … at the weekend? (go)
12. Where … you …? (be) You look very dirty.
13. … you ever … an accident? (have) Yes, I … my leg skiing a few years ago. (break)
14. How long … you … your penfriend? (know) – Well, we … writing to each other about six months ago. (start)
15. My sister is going to Italy in the summer. That is why she … to learn Italian. (start)

2 Simple past – present perfect   Wissen

§ 1 Gebrauch des simple past

§ 1	I **went** to the cinema last night. 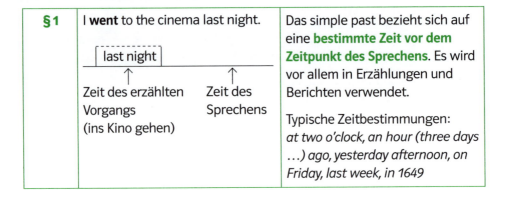	Das simple past bezieht sich auf eine **bestimmte Zeit vor dem Zeitpunkt des Sprechens**. Es wird vor allem in Erzählungen und Berichten verwendet. Typische Zeitbestimmungen: *at two o'clock, an hour (three days …) ago, yesterday afternoon, on Friday, last week, in 1649*

§ 2 Gebrauch des present perfect

Man verwendet das *present perfect* in folgenden Fällen:

§ 2.1	a) How long **have** you **been** here? (You are still here) b) I **have known** John for years. (I still do) 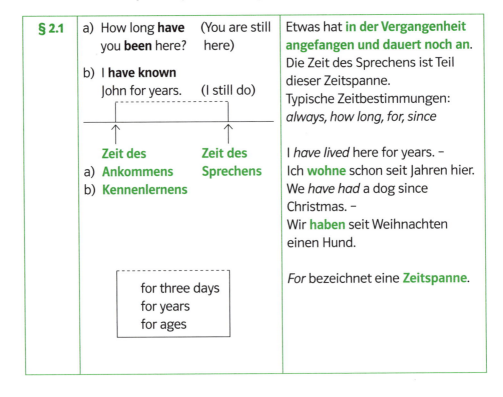	Etwas hat **in der Vergangenheit angefangen und dauert noch an**. Die Zeit des Sprechens ist Teil dieser Zeitspanne. Typische Zeitbestimmungen: *always, how long, for, since* I *have lived* here for years. – Ich **wohne** schon seit Jahren hier. We *have had* a dog since Christmas. – Wir **haben** seit Weihnachten einen Hund. *For* bezeichnet eine **Zeitspanne**.

zu § 2.1	X ⟶ since Tuesday since 2001 since we met	*Since* bezeichnet den **Ausgangspunkt** einer Handlung oder eines Vorgangs.
§ 2.2	Would you like some tea? – No, thanks. I'**ve just had** some. You **have just won** a million pounds.	Etwas ist **gerade eben geschehen**. Typische Zeitbestimmung: *just*
§ 2.3	Ann **has had** a baby. (There is a baby in the family now) **Have** you **had** a hard day? (Are you tired?) I **have seen** that film. (I know what it is about) Someone **has shot** the bank manager. (He is dead) I **have read** the newspaper. (You can throw it away)	Wir interessieren uns mehr für das **Ergebnis** als für das, was geschehen ist. Aus dem Ergebnis können Folgerungen gezogen werden, oder es sind weitere Handlungen möglich.
§ 2.4	I **have had** fish and chips several times. **Have** you ever **been** in love? Susan **hasn't kissed** me yet.	Etwas hat sich bis jetzt **einmal, mehrmals oder nie** ereignet. Typische Zeitbestimmungen: *ever, never, often, several times, yet* **Beachte:** *Ever* und *several times* werden oft mit „schon" und „schon mehrmals" übersetzt.
§ 2.5	**Have** you **heard** the news? Someone **broke** into Jean's flat. Here are the main points of the news: The Queen **has finished** her tour of Australia. She **arrived** home last night. The number of unemployed **has risen**. Another 2,000 jobs **were** lost.	**Gespräche oder Berichte** über vergangene Ereignisse werden im *present perfect* angefangen. Der genaue Zeitpunkt wird aber nicht erwähnt. Weitere Angaben (wann und wie es geschah, was darauf folgte usw.) stehen im *simple past*.

2 Simple past – present perfect   Wissen

§ 3 Zeitadverbien im present perfect und im simple past

Oft kann man an den Zeitadverbien erkennen, welche Zeitform nötig ist.

Beispiele: I have **just** had some tea. (§ 2.2)
  Have you **ever** been in love? (§ 2.4)
  I went to the cinema **last night**. (§ 1)

Manche Zeitadverbien können sowohl im **present perfect** als auch im **simple past** erscheinen. Es kommt auf die Einstellung des Sprechers zur Vergangenheit an.

Beispiele:

I **haven't had** a cold this year.	Ich habe in diesem Jahr **noch** keinen Schnupfen gehabt. (Es kann noch kommen, weil das Jahr noch nicht vorbei ist.)
I **didn't have** a cold this year.	Ich **hatte** in diesem Jahr keinen Schnupfen. (Und ich werde wahrscheinlich keinen mehr bekommen, da das Jahr fast vorbei ist.)
Susan **has** never **kissed** me.	Susan hat mich **noch nie** geküsst.
Susan never **kissed** me.	**Damals** hat mich Susan nie geküsst. (Der Sprecher denkt an eine bestimmte Zeit in der Vergangenheit.)

Beachte:
Im amerikanischen Englisch wird häufig das **simple past** verwendet, wo im britischen Englisch das **present perfect** erforderlich wäre:
AE: Did you find your key yet?
BE: Have you found your key yet?

1

Warum wird in diesem Cartoon das *present perfect* und nicht das *simple past* gebraucht? Welche Regel ist ausschlaggebend?

2

What is the difference in meaning between these sentences?

1. I have been at this school for five years.
2. I was at this school for five years.
3. Alan has worked hard this morning.
4. Alan worked hard this morning.

In welchem der folgenden Sätze denkt der Sprecher an einen bestimmten Zeitpunkt? Was deutet darauf hin?

5. Did you go on holiday with friends?
6. I have often been away with friends.
7. My brother has never lent me any money.
8. My brother wouldn't lend me any money.
9. Did you eat all the cake?
10. Who has eaten all the cake?
11. Bus fares have gone up.
12. Bus fares went up a few weeks ago.

Welche Regeln treffen für den Gebrauch des *present perfect* in den Sätzen 1–12 zu?

2 Simple past – present perfect

Übungen

No wonder we haven't had a single customer today – you forgot to unlock the doors.

3

Warum werden hier zwei verschiedene Zeiten benutzt?

Welche Regeln sind bei der Erklärung hilfreich?

4

Match up these two lists to make sentences. Use the simple past or the present perfect.

Example:

You – ride a horse? ever → **Have you ever ridden a horse?**

You – find your key? Where
I – finish my homework now
I – write four letters since two o'clock
You – go on holiday? last year
My parents – be abroad never
You – live here now? How long
You – like the film? Why not
Your penfriend – answer your letter? yet
I – hear the news just
My mother – lend me her car last night

5

A travel agency has advertised for a courier. The work involves taking tourists on guided coach tours of Europe for 2–6 weeks. They are looking for someone who can speak at least one foreign language, is confident and energetic and likes meeting people. Imagine you are the interviewer. Use the simple past or present perfect forms of the verbs.

Interviewer:	Now, Carol. What … your best subjects at school? (be)
Carol:	French and German.
Interviewer:	And you … school? (just leave)
Carol:	Yes, I left at Easter.
Interviewer:	… for any other jobs yet? (apply)
Carol:	Well, I've seen several advertised in the paper, but I haven't written yet.
Interviewer:	Who … you about this job? (tell)
Carol:	The job centre.
Interviewer:	And who … you … there? (talk to)
Carol:	Mrs Jenkins.
Interviewer:	I see. And when she … you why you … this job what … her? (ask want – tell)
Carol:	I told her I've always wanted to travel and meet lots of people.
Interviewer:	I see … ever … abroad? (be)
Carol:	Yes. Last summer I worked as an au pair in Paris.
Interviewer:	Alright, Carol. Thank you very much. Will you wait outside, please?
Interviewer:	Good morning, Mark. You're twenty minutes late. What …? (happen)
Mark:	I'm afraid I missed the bus.
Interviewer:	… late? (get up)
Mark:	No, but my mother didn't feel well, so I had to get breakfast for my little sister.
Interviewer:	I see. So that's why you … time to clean your shoes before you came out. (not have)
	Now, Mark, you … several jobs since you … school. Why? … them? (have – leave – not like)
Mark:	No, not really. I wanted something more interesting.
Interviewer:	… any foreign languages at school? (learn)
Mark:	Yes, French and Spanish.
Interviewer:	And … ever … those countries? (visit)
Mark:	Oh yes. Last summer I went camping in Spain and the year before I worked on a farm in France for six months.
Interviewer:	Alright, Mark. Thank you. Wait outside for a moment please.

Who would you give the job to and why?

Underline all the words which helped you to choose the present perfect.

3 Past progressive – simple past

Sind Sie manchmal unsicher, wann **past progressive** und wann **simple past** zu verwenden ist? Dieses Kapitel wird Ihnen helfen, diese zwei Formen auseinander zu halten.

Zuerst einige Beispiele:

past progressive	past progressive / simple past
What **were** you **doing** at about seven last night? I **was thinking** of going to town this afternoon. I **was going** to stay in tonight.	Jimmy **was dancing** on the table when the teacher **came** in. Sherlock Holmes **was sitting** in his armchair. He **was reading** a newspaper. Suddenly he **heard** footsteps.

Überprüfen Sie Ihr Wissen

Put the verbs in brackets into the simple past or past progressive.

1. It … dark when we finally … home. (get, get)
2. Have you seen my gloves? I … them when I … . (wear, arrive)
3. 'What are you doing this afternoon?' – 'I … of trying out my new camera. Do you want to help me?' (think)
4. This time last week we … still … our holiday. (enjoy)
5. We … our holiday very much. We went to Cornwall. (enjoy)
6. When the postman … the bell I … a shower. (ring, have)
7. 'Have you any plans for Saturday night?' 'Not really. I … to stay in.' (go)
8. I … the phone because I … to a CD. (not hear, listen)
9. All the time that woman … I … of something else. (talk, think)
10. I … if you could give me a lift into town? (wonder)
11. Mike said he … to talk because he … the next train. (not be able to stop, catch)
12. Mike … to talk for a minute before he … his train. (stop, catch)
13. Who … when the accident …? (drive, happen)
14. As soon as I … your letter I quickly … my breakfast … my coat … to the bus stop and here I am. (get, finish, grab, run)
15. Aunt Catherine … to see us tonight, but she can't come now because her car won't start. (come)

3 Past progressive – simple past · Wissen

§ 1 Gebrauch des past progressive

Man verwendet das **past progressive** in folgenden Fällen:

§ 1.1	What **were** you **doing** at about seven last night? ┌──────────────────┐ │ I **was listening** │ │ to the news │ └──────────────────┘ ↑ ↑ ↑ past 7.00 now	Um auszudrücken, dass eine **Handlung zu einem bestimmten Zeitpunkt in der Vergangenheit gerade vor sich ging**, d. h. noch nicht zu Ende war.
§ 1.2	'What are you doing this afternoon?' 'I **was thinking** of going to town.' („Aber wenn du einen anderen Vorschlag hast, bin ich einverstanden.") I **was thinking** of going to town this afternoon. („Willst du mitgehen?") I **was wondering** if you could lend me five pounds?	Um **höflich** zu sein: a) wenn man anderen den Eindruck geben will, dass **ihre Ideen wichtiger sind als die eigenen**, b) wenn man andere **indirekt einladen** will, c) wenn man **um etwas bitten** will.
§ 1.3	As the doctor entered the room Jane **coughed/was coughing**. A gun **fired/was firing** in the distance.	Bei Verben, die einen **kurzen und schnellen** Vorgang ausdrücken, bewirkt die *progressive form*, dass der Vorgang als **mehrere Male wiederholt** angesehen wird. Häufige Verben: *flash, kick, jump*.
§ 1.4	My girlfriend **was coming** to the party, but unfortunately she's ill. I **was going to** stay in tonight, but I've changed my mind.	**Present progressive-future in the past** (siehe Kap. 5, § 4). **Going to-future in the past** (siehe Kap. 5, § 3). Hier dreht es sich um in der Vergangenheit geplante zukünftige Handlungen, die doch nicht ausgeführt werden.

§ 2 Past progressive und simple past im Vergleich

§ 2.1	Jimmy **was dancing** on the table (1) when the teacher **came** in (2). I **was doing** when Sue **came** my homework in and kissed me. (1) (2) 〜〜〜〜● ─────→ past ↑	Das *past progressive* beschreibt, was zu einem bestimmten Zeitpunkt in der Vergangenheit gerade vorging, also die **Hintergrundshandlung** (1), als ein neues Ereignis (2) eintrat. Für das neue Ereignis verwendet man das *simple past*. **Beachte:** Einige Verben kommen normalerweise nicht in der Verlaufsform vor (vgl. Kap. *Simple present – present progressive* § 3).
§ 2.2	Ann **was trying** to do her homework, while her father **was watching** television. Ken **came** into the room, **threw** his bag on the floor and **said**, "I've decided to become a pop star."	Wenn **mehrere Vorgänge gleichzeitig im Ablauf** waren, steht in allen Fällen das *past progressive*. (Um auszudrücken, dass mehrere abgeschlossene Vorgänge aufeinander folgten, benutzt man dagegen das *simple past*).
§ 2.3	Sherlock Holmes **was sitting** in his favourite armchair. He **was reading** a newspaper and **smoking** his favourite pipe. (Hintergrundshandlungen) Suddenly he **heard** footsteps outside his door. (Neues, abgeschlossenes Ereignis)	Das *past progressive* wird häufig für **beschreibende Teile** in Erzählungen oder Berichten benutzt, d. h. zur Beschreibung von **Hintergrundshandlungen** oder **Begleitumständen**.

3 Past progressive – simple past   Übungen

1
Use the past progressive or simple past forms of the verbs in brackets to find out the story of the stolen jewels.

Lord and Lady Richmouth … (give) another of their famous parties. As usual, there were hundreds of guests. They … all … (wear) their most expensive clothes and jewelry. Everyone … (have) a wonderful time. A band … (play) and some people … (dance). Others … (stand) around in small groups … (talk) and … (laugh). Almost everyone … (eat) or … (drink) something.

Suddenly Sally Starlight, the famous film star … (scream): "Someone's stolen my necklace! Help!"

A few minutes later the Inspector … (arrive). She … (interview) all the guests in turn:

Inspector: Now, Miss Gaygirl, what … you … (do) when Miss Starlight noticed that her necklace had been stolen?
Miss G.: I … (talk) to General Blimp, wasn't I, General?
General: That's right, my dear. You … (tell) me about your new horses.
Inspector: And what about you, Mr Steel? What … you … (do)?
Mr Steel: I … (dance) with Mrs Heavyfoot. I danced with her all night, without stopping.
Inspector: Is that right, Mrs Heavyfoot?
Mrs H.: Well, yes. That is – no, not quite. Just before Miss Starlight cried out he left the room.
Inspector: What? Hey, come back! He's running away.

2

Put these two lists together. Explain the difference between each pair of sentences.

1. a) When I got to the party
   b) When I got to the party
2. a) What were you doing when the lights went out?
   b) What did you do when the lights went out?
3. a) The girl was drowning …
   b) The girl drowned …
4. a) When the phone rang …
   b) When the phone rang …
5. a) When I looked at the baby …
   b) When I looked at the baby …
6. a) What did you do when your brother fell into the river?
   b) What were you doing when your brother fell into the river?

- I lit a candle.
- I got out of the bath and answered it.
- I was having a bath, so I couldn't answer it.
- it was crying.
- I jumped in after him.
- it cried.
- I was having a shower.
- I was just a few metres away, fishing.
- everyone went home.
- They couldn't save her.
- everyone was going home.
- but they saved her.

3 Past progressive – simple past   Übungen

3

Use the past progressive or simple past forms of the verbs in brackets to complete these sentences.

1. At nine o'clock we … still … for Tony. (wait)
2. When we finally … at the station the train … just … . (arrive, leave)
3. 'Are you doing anything at the weekend?' 'Well, I … to go to the football match, but if you want to do anything else I don't mind.' (plan)
4. Who … you … to when I … you yesterday? (talk, see)
5. We … the cathedral because it … . (not be able to visit, repair)
6. This time last year we … exams. (do)
7. We … of going to the disco. Would you like to come? (think)
8. '… Johnny last night? He … black tights and a fur coat.' (you see, wear)
9. When it … to rain everyone who … the match … up an umbrella. (start, watch, put)
10. 'I thought you … out tonight?' 'I was, but my car won't start.' (go)
11. When Judy … the burglar she … the door … into the cellar and … a hammer. (hear, lock, run, fetch)
12. While Kevin … in England he … a very nice girl. (stay, meet)
13. My car won't start. I … if you could give me a hand? (wonder)

4

Use the past progressive and simple past forms once each to complete each pair of sentences.

Example:

Sally – listen to the news – while – have a bath.
Sally listened to the news while she was having a bath.

Sally – listen to the news – then – have a bath.
Sally listened to the news, then she had a bath.

1. a) When – the teacher – walk in – pupils – listen to music and dance.
   b) When – the teacher – walk in – pupils – stop dancing.

2. a) Linda – go home by taxi – because – miss – last bus.
   b) John – go home by taxi – because – rain so hard.

3. a) I – not hear the announcement – because – somebody – talk.
   b) I – not hear the announcement – because – somebody – switch the radio off.

5

Write the story, using the past progressive and simple past.
Find your own ending.

You chaps seen any reindeers pass this way?

One day Santa Claus – not find – reindeers. So – go out – look for. It – snow.
Suddenly – meet two men. They – sit next to a fire. On the fire – saucepan – food
in it. The men – eat some meat. The meat – look like Santa's reindeers. When
Santa – see what the men – eat he …

4 Present perfect progressive – present perfect simple – past perfect

Die richtige Anwendung des *present perfect progressive* ist nicht ganz einfach. Aber keine Angst!
Wenn Sie dieses Kapitel durchgearbeitet haben, werden Sie hoffentlich keine Fehler mehr machen.

Einige Beispiele:

present perfect simple	present perfect progressive
I **have** never **danced** with Keith.	We **have been dancing** all night.
Tina **has told** me about her holidays.	Tina **has been talking** for hours.
Julie **has painted** a picture.	Julie **has been painting** all day.
Someone **has eaten** my biscuits.	Someone **has been eating** my biscuits.
I**'ve cleaned** the whole flat.	I**'ve been cleaning** all morning.
Have you **played** tennis before?	How long **have** you **been playing** tennis?
Angela **has learnt** to ski.	Angela **has been learning** to ski for years.
Which countries **have** you **lived** in?	I**'ve been living** in America since 2003.

past perfect
Kevin didn't go to the cinema with us because he **had seen** the film before.
If you **had asked** me I would have lent you some money.

Prüfen Sie nach, ob Sie diese Formen richtig anwenden können.

Überprüfen Sie Ihr Wissen

1

Complete these sentences by using the simple or progressive forms of the present perfect.

1. I ... my homework. (do) Now I can go out.
2. I ... my homework for three hours. (do)
3. 'What ... you ... all afternoon?' (do) 'I ... that book you lent me (read), but I ... it yet.' (not finish)
4. Esmeralda is a famous film star. She ... films since she was sixteen. She ... about ten films. (make, make)
5. How long ... Jill ... (go) out with Ron?
6. How long ... Jill and Ron ... each other? (know)
7. Sue ... to ring you all morning. (try)
8. Sue ... to ring you several times. (try)
9. I ... always ... English. (like)

2

These sentences are all wrong. They are typical mistakes made by Germans. Can you correct them?

1. It is raining all day.
2. How long are you waiting for me?
3. I am knowing my girlfriend for three months.
4. Julie has painted all day.
5. How long do you learn English? You're very good.
6. Your eyes are red. Have you cried?
7. I'm tired. I've worked very hard today.
8. Sally has been having a cold for ages.
9. We have been living here since two years.

4 Pres. perf. progr. – pres. perf. simple – past perf. — Wissen

§ 1 Gebrauch des present perfect progressive

Das *present perfect progressive* wird verwendet:

§ 1.1	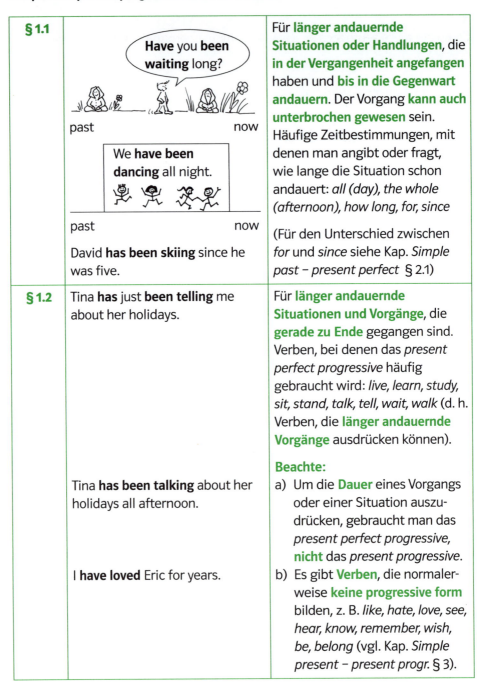 Have you been waiting long? past — now We have been dancing all night. past — now David has been skiing since he was five.	Für **länger andauernde Situationen oder Handlungen**, die **in der Vergangenheit angefangen** haben und **bis in die Gegenwart andauern**. Der Vorgang **kann auch unterbrochen gewesen** sein. Häufige Zeitbestimmungen, mit denen man angibt oder fragt, wie lange die Situation schon andauert: *all (day), the whole (afternoon), how long, for, since* (Für den Unterschied zwischen *for* und *since* siehe Kap. *Simple past – present perfect* § 2.1)
§ 1.2	Tina **has** just **been telling** me about her holidays. Tina **has been talking** about her holidays all afternoon. I **have loved** Eric for years.	Für **länger andauernde Situationen und Vorgänge**, die **gerade zu Ende** gegangen sind. Verben, bei denen das *present perfect progressive* häufig gebraucht wird: *live, learn, study, sit, stand, talk, tell, wait, walk* (d. h. Verben, die **länger andauernde Vorgänge** ausdrücken können). **Beachte:** a) Um die **Dauer** eines Vorgangs oder einer Situation auszudrücken, gebraucht man das *present perfect progressive*, **nicht** das *present progressive*. b) Es gibt **Verben**, die normalerweise **keine progressive form** bilden, z. B. *like, hate, love, see, hear, know, remember, wish, be, belong* (vgl. Kap. *Simple present – present progr.* § 3).

Das **present progressive** *(I am doing)* wird oft fälschlicherweise anstelle des **present perfect progressive** *(I have been doing)* verwendet. Die nächste Übung hilft Ihnen, diesen Fehler zu vermeiden.

1

Translate the following sentences, using the present progressive or present perfect progressive.

1. Es regnet.
2. Es regnet schon seit heute morgen.
3. Mr Williams redet schon eine Stunde lang.
4. Mr Williams redet über seine Operation.
5. Meine Freundin lernt Italienisch.
6. Seit sechs Monaten lernt meine Freundin Italienisch.

Look at the English translations. Which two words show you when you need the present perfect progressive form?

2

Complete each sentence in two different ways, using 'for' and 'since'. The following words will help you: (two) o'clock, (three) hours, half an hour, ten minutes, six months, breakfast, (he) came home (from school), March …

1. Dad … (make) dinner   since …
                                 for …
2. Grandad … (sing)   since …
                                 for …
3. My boyfriend … (work) on his computer   since …
                                 for …
4. Kevin … (look) for a job   since …
                                 for …

4 Pres. perf. progr. – pres. perf. simple – past perf. — Wissen

§ 2 Present perfect simple und present perfect progressive im Vergleich

	present perfect, simple form	
	Julie **has painted** a picture.	
§ 2.1	I **have read** that book you lent me. (Now I know what it is about.) I**'ve cleaned** the whole flat. (The flat is clean now.)	Eine Tätigkeit ist beendet und hat ein Ergebnis. Wir interessieren uns besonders für dieses **Ergebnis**.
§ 2.2	I **have often danced** with Keith. Sally **has played** table-tennis **hundreds of times**.	Wir interessieren uns dafür, **wie häufig** eine Tätigkeit ausgeführt wurde *(ten times, often, never …)*.

	present perfect, progressive form	
	Julie **has been painting**.	
§ 2.1.1	'What have you been doing all day?' – 'I **have been reading** that book you lent me.'	Eine Tätigkeit ist noch nicht beendet und hat noch kein Ergebnis. Wir interessieren uns ausschließlich für die **Tätigkeit**.
§ 2.1.2	I'm tired. **I've been cleaning** my flat all day. (That's why I'm tired.)	Die Tätigkeit hatte eine Folge. Wir interessieren uns eher dafür, **wie es zu dieser Folge kam** als für die Folge selber.
§ 2.2	Keith **has been dancing all evening**. Sally **has been playing** table-tennis **since she could walk**.	Wir interessieren uns dafür, **wie lange** eine Tätigkeit ausgeführt wurde. Die Tätigkeit kann ununterbrochen oder mit Unterbrechungen ausgeführt worden sein. **Beachte:** Die deutschen Entsprechungen des *present perfect progressive*: *What have you been doing lately?* (= Was **hast** du in der letzten Zeit **gemacht**?) *I have been waiting for ages.* (= Ich **warte** schon ewig.)

4 Pres. perf. progr. – pres. perf. simple – past perf. — Übungen

3

Read the situation, then write two sentences, one with the simple and one with the progressive form of the present perfect.

Example:
Karin collects stamps. She started collecting them two years ago.
(She/collect stamps/two years)   She has been collecting stamps for two years.
(She/collect/about two thousand) She has collected about two thousand.

1. Don can drive a car. He took the test six months ago.
   (He/drive/six months) …
   (He/drive/about five thousand kilometres) …
2. 'You look slimmer than the last time I saw you.'
   (Yes, I/slim) '…'
   (Yes, I/lose/a lot of weight) '…'
3. 'Have you been helping Alan with his homework?'
   (Yes, I/explain something to him) '…'
   (Oh, I/explain it so often/but/still can't do it) '…'

Which rules helped you to answer these questions?

4

Imagine you are talking to some friends. Ask questions with 'How long', 'How many' and 'How often'. Use the simple or progressive forms of the present perfect.

Example:
Your friend is learning French.   How long have you been learning French?

1. Your friend is waiting for you.   …?
2. Your friend collects stamps.   How long …?
                                         How many …?
3. Trevor is on holiday.   …? (be on holiday)
4. Your friend is smoking.   How long …?
                                         How many … today?
5. Your friend has a cold.   …?
6. Your friend has borrowed one   before you borrow anything? (tell you to ask
   of your books without asking.   me)

'How long' ist ein Signalwort für das …
Ausnahmen: Verben, wie … (Frage …), … (Frage …), … die normalerweise keine
… bilden. (Vgl. § …).

5
Can you match up these lists?

1. I have had six cups of tea already.
2. I have been drinking tea all day.
3. Charlie has drunk eight pints of beer.
4. Charlie has been drinking.
5. I have been walking to school all week.
6. I have often walked to school.
7. Dennis has been spending a lot of money lately.
8. Dennis has spent a lot of money on his motor bike.

The buses were on strike.

I wonder where he got it from?

Haven't you?

And your mother has just poured me a seventh.

Have you seen it?

Now he can't stand up.

There was nothing else to do.

I could never drink so many.

§ 3 Present perfect progressive und simple past im Vergleich

present perfect progressive	simple past
David **has been skiing since** he was five.	**When did** he **start** skiing? He **started when he was five**.
Angela **has been playing** the guitar **for** years.	Angela **learnt** to play the guitar **years ago**.
How long has Sheila **been going** out with Tom?	Sheila **asked** Tom to go out with her about **two weeks ago**.
Wenn man sich eher dafür interessiert, **wie lange** eine Situation oder ein Vorgang schon andauert, benutzt man das *present perfect progressive*. Häufige Zeitbestimmungen: *how long, for, since*.	Wenn man sagen oder fragen will, **wann** etwas passiert ist, benutzt man das *simple past*.

§ 4 Simple past, present perfect simple und progressive form im Überblick

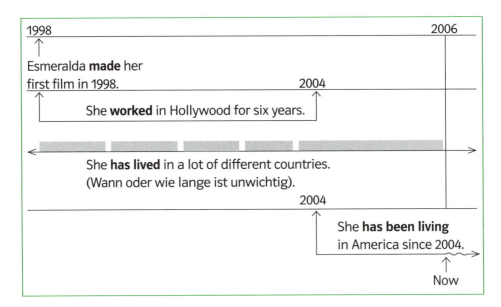

6

Ask questions with 'how long' and 'when'.

1. Lynne is learning judo.
   (How long/she/learn judo?) …
   (When/she/start learning judo?) …

2. Marion is waiting for Dennis.
   (How long/she/wait?) …
   (When/she/arrive?) …

3. Mike is working in Glasgow.
   (How long/he/work there?) …
   (When/he/leave Wales?) …

7

Mr Gambol has hurt his finger.

Mrs Gambol: (How/you/do it?) …
Mr Gambol: (use/my pocket calculator/all day) …

4 Pres. perf. progr. – pres. perf. simple – past perf. — Übungen

8

It is Saturday. Mike doesn't go to work on Saturdays, but he does a lot of other things. Today he was very busy.

From 9.00 to 10.00 he cleaned his flat.
At 10.00 he did some washing.
At 10.30 he made a cake.
At 11.00 he started to paint a cupboard.
From 11.45 to 12.15 he practised the guitar.
At 12.15 he had lunch.

After lunch he read the paper, then washed the pots.
From 13.30 to 14.00 he wrote some letters.
From 14.00 to 15.00 he played table tennis.
From 15.30 to 16.00 he put his holiday photos into an album.
At 16.00 he started doing the ironing.
At 17.00 he had tea.
At 18.00 he fell asleep.
Now it's 20.00. He was so tired he's still asleep!

Can you talk about what Mike did today?

Example:
It's 10.00. Mike **has cleaned** his flat. He **started** at nine and he**'s been cleaning for** an hour.

It's 10.30. Mike … some washing. He … at 10.00 and he … it … half an hour.
It's 11.10. Mike … a cake and he … to … a cupboard. He … it since 11.00.
It's 12.15. Mike … to … half an hour ago. He has … 11.45.
It's 14.00. Mike … his lunch. After that he … the pots. He … letters … half an hour.
It's 14.45. Mike has … 14.00.
It's 16.30. Mike … his holiday photos into an album. Now he … the ironing. He … half an hour.
Now it's 19.00. Mike … his tea and … asleep. He … asleep … 18.00.

§ 5 Gebrauch des past perfect

Das *past perfect* wird verwendet für:

§ 5.1	Jeff **had** already **bought** the tickets when Sue said she wasn't going. Kevin didn't go to the cinema with us because he **had seen** the film before. When I arrived at the party most people **had left**. (Vgl.: When I arrived most people **left**!)	Ein **Geschehen**, das **vor** einem bestimmten **Zeitpunkt in der Vergangenheit** stattgefunden hat.
§ 5.2	I was very surprised. I **hadn't seen** a camel before.	Einen **Zustand**, der **vor** einem bestimmten **Zeitpunkt in der Vergangenheit** begann und zu diesem Zeitpunkt noch **andauerte**.
§ 5.3	How long **had** you **been waiting** when your boyfriend finally arrived? We **had** only **been talking** for a few minutes when my bus came.	Wenn eine Handlung oder ein Zustand **bis** zu einem **Zeitpunkt der Vergangenheit** noch **andauerte** und **Ablauf** oder **Dauer** besonders **betont** werden sollen, wird die *progressive form* gebraucht.
§ 5.4	Jane phoned all her friends to tell them that she **had passed** her exams.	Das *past perfect* wird oft in der **indirekten Rede** verwendet. (Vgl. Kap. *Indirect speech* § 4.2)
§ 5.5	**If** you **had asked** me I would have lent you some money. I **wish** I **had worked** harder for the exams.	Nach *if, if only* und *wish* drückt das *past perfect* aus, dass etwas **nicht eingetreten** ist. (Vgl. Kap. *If-clauses* § 5)

5 Future time

Im Englischen gibt es viele Möglichkeiten, über die Zukunft zu reden. Die Wahl der richtigen Form hängt davon ab, was man ausdrücken will. Hier zunächst eine Übersicht über die Zukunftsformen:

We **won't be** back before tea.	**will-future**
That plane **is going** to crash.	**going to-future**
Dorothy **is working** next Saturday.	**present progressive-future**
What time **does** the film **start**?	**simple present-future**
I'll ring you when I **get** home.	**simple present-future after 'if, when …'**
I'll be playing football between four and five.	**future progressive**
The concert **won't have finished** by nine.	**future perfect**
By six o' clock Sue **will have been dancing** for 48 hours.	**future perfect progressive**

Das sieht zunächst vielleicht etwas verwirrend aus. Aber nur keine Angst! Prüfen Sie erst einmal nach, was Sie schon können.

Überprüfen Sie Ihr Wissen

Choose the correct future forms to complete these sentences.

1. 'Can you come tomorrow night?' 'Sorry, I … table tennis.'
   (play/will play/am playing)
2. What time … the concert …?
   (does … end/will … end)
3. If you … here by seven I'll leave without you.
   (aren't/won't be)
4. The sun is coming out. It … be a nice day.
   (is going to/will)
5. Do you think the world … a better place in 100 years time?
   (is/will be)
6. 'I can't open this tin.' 'I … do it for you.'
   (am going to/will)
7. What do you want to do when you … school?
   (leave/will leave)
8. Diana has changed her job. Now she … work with computers.
   (is going to/will)
9. Don't come before five. I … my homework.
   (will do/will be doing)
10. By this time next week I … all my exams.
    (will finish/will have finished)
11. By ten o'clock I … for four hours.
    (will have worked/will have been working)

5 Future time

Wissen

§ 1 Übersicht über die verschiedenen Futurformen

will	– künftiges Geschehen, das der Sprecher nicht beeinflussen kann	It **will** soon be dark.	§ 2.1
	– Vermutungen und Voraussagen	We **won't be** back before tea.	§ 2.2
	– spontane Entschlüsse und Versprechen	I**'ll help** you.	§ 2.3
going to	– fester Vorsatz	Jill **is going to** be an engineer.	§ 3.1
	– Schlussfolgerungen aus der Gegenwart	That plane **is going to** crash.	§ 3.2
present progressive	– fest beschlossener, vereinbarter Plan, meist mit Zeitangabe	Dorothy **is working** on Saturday.	§ 4
simple present	– künftiges Geschehen als Teil eines Fahrplans/festgelegten Programms	What time **does** the film **start**?	§ 5.1
	– Bedingungen nach *if, when*	I'll ring you when I **get** home.	§ 5.2
future progressive	– Vorgang, der zu einem bestimmten Zeitpunkt in der Zukunft (noch) abläuft	Don't ring between 4 and 5. I**'ll be playing** football.	§ 6.1
	– üblicherweise eintretendes Geschehen	I**'ll be passing** the letter box anyway.	§ 6.2
	– Erkundigungen, ohne neugierig oder aufdringlich zu wirken	**Will** you **be paying** cash?	§ 6.3
future perfect simple	– Aussagen oder Erkundigungen darüber, ob ein Vorgang zu einem bestimmten Zeitpunkt in der Zukunft abgeschlossen sein wird oder nicht, immer mit Zeitbestimmung	The concert **won't have finished** by nine.	§ 7.1
future perfect progressive	– Vorgang, der zu einem bestimmten Zeitpunkt in der Zukunft schon seit einiger Zeit andauert, von der Zukunft aus gesehen	By six o'clock Sue **will have been dancing** for 48 hours.	§ 7.2

§ 2 Das will-future

Manchmal wird *shall* anstatt *will* verwendet, aber nur mit *I* oder *we*.

We **shall/will** probably have a class party next week.
I **shan't/won't** be here tomorrow.

Will ist häufiger als *shall*. *Shall* wird vorwiegend für **Vorschläge und Angebote** benutzt:

Shall I open the window?
Where **shall** we go tonight?

Im gesprochenen Englisch hört man in Aussagesätzen meistens nur die Kurzform *'ll*.

Das **will-future** wird verwendet für:

§ 2.1	It **will** soon **be** dark. I**'ll be** eighteen next year.	Künftiges Geschehen, das der **Sprecher nicht beeinflussen kann**.
§ 2.2	Do you **think** Carol **will get** the job? My father **won't like** my new hairstyle. We **probably won't be** back before ten. I **expect** we**'ll find** the way.	**Vermutungen und Voraussagen**, oft nach *be sure, expect, imagine, suppose, think, perhaps, probably.* Im Deutschen ist es meist unwichtig, ob man das Präsens (wir finden den Weg) oder das Futur (wir werden den Weg finden) benutzt. Im Englischen muss man in solchen Fällen das *will-future* verwenden (nicht das *simple present*).
§ 2.3	I**'ll meet** you in half an hour. I**'ll help** you with your homework. I **won't be** long.	**Spontane Entschlüsse und Versprechen.** Hier steht im Deutschen meist die Gegenwart (Wir treffen uns …).

Beachte:
I will = ich werde
ich will = I want

5 Future time

Wissen

§ 3 Das going to-future

Wir verwenden *going to* für:

§ 3.1	What **are** you **going to** do when you leave school? Jill **is going to** be an engineer.	**Künftige Ereignisse**, über die wir uns **vorher bereits Gedanken** gemacht haben und zu einem **festen Entschluss** gekommen sind.
§ 3.2	Marion **is going to** have a baby. Look at that plane. It's **going to** land.	**Schlussfolgerungen** aus einem gegenwärtigen Zustand.

Beachte:
Bei den Verben *go* und *come* wird aus stilistischen Gründen normalerweise keine *going to progressive*-Form gebraucht. Statt dessen steht das *present progressive*:

We**'re going** on holiday in July. (nicht *going to go*)
Are you **coming** to the party tonight? (nicht *going to come*)

1

1. Jenny has just written a letter, but she can't find an envelope.
   Jenny: Linda, we haven't got any envelopes, have we?
   Linda: No, but I'm just going out. I**'ll** get some.
   Before she goes she talks to Carol.
   Linda: I**'m going to** get some envelopes. Can I get you anything, Carol?

In welchem Satz
a) wird der Entschluss erst im Moment des Sprechens gefasst?
b) wurde der Entschluss vor dem Moment des Sprechens gefasst?

Überlegen Sie bei den folgenden Sätzen, ob eine spontane Äußerung oder ein fester Entschluss vorliegt, und vervollständigen Sie dann bitte die Sätze.

2. Diane: My car won't start. I'll be late for work.
   Sue: Don't worry. I … take you.
   A few minutes later Sue talks to her husband.
   Sue: I … take Diane to work. Her car won't start.
3. Helen: Can you mend my bike, Dad?
   Father: Alright, but not just now. I … do it later.
4. Mrs Smith: Bill, has Helen told you about her bike?
   Mr Smith: Yes, I … do it later.
5. John: Are you going shopping?
   Alan: Yes, I … buy something for tea.
6. Dave: I don't know how to use this camera.
   Janet: It's easy. I … show you.

2

Fill in 'will' or 'going to' and say which rule helped you.

1. Kevin hasn't done any work for his exam. He … fail.
2. 'Do you think you … pass the exam?' 'I don't know, but I … try very hard.'
3. 'What would you like to drink?' 'I … have a coffee, please.'
4. You'd better put your coat on. It … be cold.
5. 'Where … spend your holidays this year?' 'I expect we … go to France, as usual.'
6. Look at that stupid driver. There … be an accident.
7. Oh no! I've no money left. I … have to walk home.
8. I'm sure Bob … come if you ask him.
9. When … invite Bob to your party?
10. Soon there … be many wild animals left on the earth.

5 Future time

Wissen　Übungen

§ 4 Das present progressive-future

Die **present progressive**-Form kann auch benutzt werden, um über die Zukunft zu sprechen:

§ 4	Dorothy **is working** on Saturday. What time **are** you **meeting** Jill?	Das *present progressive* drückt einen **fest beschlossenen, vereinbarten Plan** aus, meist mit **Zeitangabe**.

Prüfen Sie, ob Ihnen der Unterschied zwischen *going to* und dem *present progressive* klar ist.

3
Cross out the wrong forms and say why.

1. It is raining/going to rain tomorrow.
2. You're falling/going to fall if you're not careful.

4
Which of these sentences makes the better excuse? Why?

1. I can't come on Saturday. I'm meeting Jill.
2. I can't come on Saturday. I'm going to meet Jill.

§ 5 Das simple present-future

Das *simple present* mit futurischer Bedeutung wird benutzt für:

§ 5.1	What time **does** the film **start**? The school holidays **begin** next Thursday. Tomorrow **is** Wednesday.	Zukünftiges Geschehen, das durch **Termine, Fahrplan, Programm** usw, bereits festgelegt ist; häufig bei Verben wie *begin, start, end, open, close, leave, arrive*.
§ 5.2	Will your parents be angry **if** you**'re** late? I'll ring you **when** I **get** home. Think carefully **before** you **answer** this question. **If** it **rains** we'll go by bus. (Im Deutschen würde man die Gegenwart benutzen: Wenn es **regnet**, **fahren** wir mit dem Bus.)	**Bedingungen**, die mit *if* eingeleitet werden; in **Nebensätzen** nach *when, before, until, till, as soon as*.

Beachte:
if = wenn (etwas wird **vielleicht** geschehen)
when = wenn, als (etwas wird **bestimmt** geschehen)

I'll come when **I've finished**. (nicht *will have finished*)

5 Future time

5

Finish each sentence so that it means the same as the one before.

Example:
The train leaves at five and arrives at seven.
If you **leave** at five you **will arrive** at seven.

1. People who eat too much get fat.
   If you ... too much you ... fat.
2. Careful drivers do not have accidents.
   If you ... carefully you ... an accident.
3. There are lots of interesting things to see in London.
   You ... lots of interesting things when you ... to London.
4. Orders only take a few days.
   If you ... the book it ... here in a few days.

6

Put in 'if' or 'when'. Check rule § 5.2 again first.

1. Ben might phone ... he does, tell him I'll ring back.
2. We'll go by bus ... you don't want to walk.
3. Shall we go for a coffee ... we've finished?
4. Margaret will notice a lot of changes ... she gets home.
5. ... we're not there by ten don't wait.
6. What are you going to be ... you grow up?

7

Fill in 'if' or 'when' to find out what the cartoon says.
Which rule explains why the man uses the future form 'going to'?

And tell him … he does it again
I'm going to keep it!

8

Put the verbs into the simple present or present progressive future forms.

1. The pop concert … (start) at half past seven.
2. Jenny … (have) a party next Saturday.
3. Tony, we … (go) to the disco … (you/come) with us?
4. What time … (your friend/come)?
5. What time … (the bus/leave)?

5 Future time

§ 6 Das future progressive

Das *future progressive* wird verwendet für:

§ 6.1	Don't come between 5 and 6. We'**ll be having** tea. I wonder if it **will** still **be raining** this afternoon.	Vorgänge von **begrenzter Dauer**, die zu einem bestimmten Zeitpunkt in der Zukunft **(noch) im Verlauf** sind. **Beachte:** When I get home I'll have tea. *I'll have tea* erfolgt **nach** dem Heimkommen.
§ 6.2	I'll post that letter for you. I'**ll be passing** the letter box anyway. The shops **will be closing** in half an hour.	Vorgänge, die **üblicherweise** eintreten, ohne besonders geplant zu sein, häufig mit *anyway*.
§ 6.3	**Will** you **be seeing** Tony when you go to Wales? **Will** you **be paying** cash or by cheque?	**Erkundigungen** nach einem Vorhaben klingen **nicht so neugierig oder aufdringlich**, wenn sie im *future progressive* ausgedrückt werden.

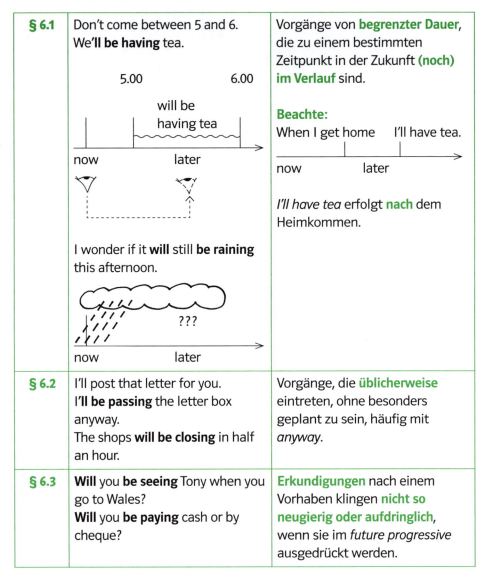

So viele Möglichkeiten, über die Zukunft zu reden! Prüfen Sie nach, ob Sie auch diese neue Möglichkeit richtig nutzen können.

9

Make sentences with 'will be ... ing'!

1. I'm going to a computer programming course tonight. It starts at 7.30 and ends at 10.00. So from 7.30 to 10.00 I ... (learn) to program computers.
2. My piano lesson is from 4 till 5. So at half past four I ... (play) the piano.
3. My homework will take at least three hours. It's five o'clock now, so at seven I ... (still/work).

Which rule explains why we use the future progressive in these sentences?

10

Steve: I have to go to town tomorrow afternoon, but there's something wrong with my bike. And it's so difficult with the buses.
Carol: That's no problem. **I'll be driving** into town anyway. I'll take you.

Steve könnte weiterfragen: 'Are you driving back?' oder 'Will you be driving back?' Was ist der Unterschied?

Ask for help in a similar way in the following situations.

1. You want to use your friend's bike tomorrow afternoon.
   ... your bike tomorrow afternoon? (you/use)
2. Your friend is going shopping. You want some stamps from the post office.
   ...? (pass/post office)

Now offer to help.

3. 'I have to give a message to Don, but he isn't on the phone.'
   'That's no problem. I ... .' (see/this afternoon).
4. 'I need some eggs, but I can't leave the house.'
   'That's ... I ... .' (go shopping/soon).

5 Future time

§ 7 Das future perfect simple und progressive

Das *future perfect* wird benutzt für:

§ 7.1	Simple form		
	The concert **won't have finished** by nine. The concert **will have started** by the time we arrive. **Will** the concert **have finished** by ten? It won't have finished It will have started now — later		Aussagen oder Erkundigung darüber, ob ein Vorgang zu einem bestimmten Zeitpunkt in der Zukunft **abgeschlossen sein wird oder nicht**, immer mit der Zeitbestimmung.
§ 7.2	Progressive form		
	By six o'clock Sue **will have been dancing** for 48 hours. now 6.00		Vorgänge, die zu einem bestimmten Zeitpunkt in der Zukunft **schon seit einiger Zeit andauern, von der Zukunft aus gesehen**. **Beachte:** At six Sue **will** still **be dancing**. (Von der Gegenwart aus gesehen: man weiß noch nicht, wie lange es dauern wird.) By six Sue **will have been dancing** for 48 hours. (Von der Zukunft aus gesehen: man weiß, wie lange es schon gedauert hat.)

11
Explain in German the differences between these sentences. Which rules help you to explain?

1. I'll fly to America next summer.
2. I am going to fly to America next summer.
3. I am flying to America next summer.
4. I fly to America next summer.
5. I'll be flying to America next summer.

12
The youth club have got a new room. What do you think they will have done to make it nicer two months from now?

13
Choose the correct future form to complete these sentences. Write down the number of the rule which helped you.

1. John can't come on Sunday. He ... his girlfriend to decorate. (will help/is helping)
2. I'm sure you ... your exam. (will pass/are passing)
3. Caroline ... for the school team on Friday. (will play/is playing)
4. The weather ... better tomorrow. (gets/will get/is getting)
5. When ... the shops ...? (do ... close/will ... close)
6. 'I haven't got enough money for the bus.' 'It's ok. I ... you some.' (am going to lend/will lend)
7. We won't catch the bus if we ... hurry. (don't/won't)
8. How long ... you ...? (do ... stay/are ... staying)
9. I ... my homework by seven. (will finish/will have finished)
10. This time next year I won't be at school. I ... . (will work/will be working)
11. The last bus ... at 11.30. (is leaving/leaves/will leave)
12. Shall we go for a coffee when the film ... over? (is/will be)
13. In five years time I probably ... with my parents any more. (won't live/won't be living)
14. Don't ring after eleven because I ... to bed. (will go/will have gone)
15. If the bus ... soon we'll have to get a taxi. (won't come/doesn't come)
16. What time ... the train ...? (does ... arrive/will ... arrive)

6 Modals

Was sind **modale Hilfsverben**, und wozu braucht man sie?

Modale Hilfsverben sind sehr wichtig, um **Einstellungen** zu bekunden, z. B. um auszudrücken, dass etwas **möglich, notwendig, empfehlenswert** ist, oder um **eine bestehende oder mangelnde Bereitschaft** zu zeigen. Der Satz *Mike ... ring his girlfriend* kann z. B. mehrere ganz verschiedene Bedeutungen haben, je nachdem, welches modale Hilfsverb eingesetzt wird:

Mike ... ring his girlfriend.	Mike **might** ring her.
	Mike **has to** ring her.
	Mike **should** ring her.
	Mike **shouldn't** ring her.
	Mike **ought to** ring her.
	Mike **won't** ring her.

Der Unterschied ist doch sehr wichtig, oder nicht?
Fällt es Ihnen leicht, die verschiedenen Bedeutungen der modalen Hilfsverben richtig zu interpretieren und auch anzuwenden? Prüfen Sie erst einmal nach, was Sie schon können.

Überprüfen Sie Ihr Wissen

1

Complete the following sentences, using 'be able to, can't have, could have, might be (-ing), might have, must, must be (-ing), must have, should be (-ing), shouldn't have'. Use each once only.

Example:
Mary's car is still outside. I don't think she **can have gone** to work.

1. Mary's car is still outside. She … to work. (go)
2. The curtains are drawn. Carol … still … in bed. (be)
3. The windows are shut. Brian … out. (go)
4. The Brands are taking suitcases to their car. They … on holiday. (go)
5. 'Do you know where Leslie is?' 'I'm not sure. She … to the youth club. Have you looked there?' (go)
6. 'Do you know where Leslie is?' 'I'm not sure. She … table-tennis.' (play)
7. I'm so tired this morning. I … so late last night. (stay up)
8. What is Kay doing here? She … her homework. (do)
9. My sister is learning Spanish. When we go on holiday next year she … it. (speak)
10. 'Did you go to Joe's party?' 'No, I …, but I didn't want to.' (go)

2

Translate the following sentences into English.

1. „Hättest du Lust, schwimmen zu gehen?"
   „Nein, ich mag jetzt nicht."
2. Soll ich dir eine Zeitung mitbringen?
3. „Ich muss jeden Tag um sieben aufstehen."
   „Ich brauche nicht so früh aufzustehen."
4. Leider konnte ich gestern nicht anrufen. Ich musste weg.
5. Unsere Freunde sollten morgen ankommen.
6. Unsere Freunde hätten gestern ankommen sollen.
7. Ich werde versuchen, deinen alten Kassettenrekorder zu reparieren. Das dürfte nicht allzu schwierig sein.
8. Du brauchst nicht einkaufen zu gehen. Ich habe alles mitgebracht.
9. Mit diesem Schnupfen darfst nicht einkaufen gehen.
10. Mit diesem Schnupfen solltest du nicht einkaufen gehen.

War das schwierig? Dieses Kapitel wird Ihnen helfen, in Zukunft keine Fehler mehr zu machen.

6 Modals

Wissen

§ 1 Can – could – could have;
can't – can't have – couldn't have; be able to

		can	
	§ 1.1	**Can** you use a computer? (= Do you know how to?) I **can't** ride a bike.	**Vorhandene** oder nicht vorhandene **Fähigkeiten**.
	§ 1.2	**Can** I use your computer? (= Will you allow me to?) – No, you **can't**.	**Erlaubnis erbitten und erteilen** oder **vorenthalten**. Unklarheiten werden durch Umschreibung mit *know how to, allow, be able to* usw. vermieden.
	§ 1.3	England **can** be very warm in summer.	**Allgemeine oder gegenwärtige Möglichkeiten.**
	§ 1.4	**Can** I get you a coffee? I **can** baby-sit for you tonight, if you like.	**Vorschläge, Angebote.**
		could	
	§ 1.5	Jane **could** read when she was four. We **couldn't** understand what Frank wanted to say.	**Fähigkeiten**, die man in der **Vergangenheit** besessen hat oder nicht. (Siehe „**Beachte**", *able to*: § 1.12)
	§ 1.6	There **could** be another rise in the price of petrol soon.	**Zukünftige Möglichkeit.**
	§ 1.7	**Could** I use your phone?	**Höfliche Fragen und Bitten.** *Could* klingt höflicher und nicht so auf dringlich wie *can*.
	§ 1.8	We **could** go on holiday together.	**Vorschläge.**
		could have	
	§ 1.9	Why didn't you ring? We **could have** met you at the station.	Etwas ist **nicht geschehen**, **obwohl** die **Gelegenheit** oder **Fähigkeit** vorhanden war.

	can't – can't have – couldn't have; be able to	
§ 1.10	Jane **can't** be ill. I saw her at the swimming pool half an hour ago. Tony **can't have** enjoyed the match. He looks very miserable.	**Logische Schlussfolgerung**: etwas ist **unmöglich**. *Can't* – siehe § 2.3; § 3.
§ 1.11	At last we **were able to/ managed to** persuade/ **succeeded in persuading** Cathy to come on holiday with us, but we **couldn't** persuade Eric. **Could** you persuade Eric to go with you last year?	In **Aussagesätzen**, die ausdrücken, dass etwas in der **Vergangenheit gelungen** ist, wird *could* durch *be able, succeed in* oder *manage to* ersetzt. In **Fragen** und **verneinten** Sätzen dagegen kann *could* verwendet werden.
§ 1.12	I'**ve** never **been able to** do maths. When I've finished this course I'**ll be able to** speak Spanish, hopefully. **Are** you **able to** drive your mother's car? **Can** you drive your mother's car? a) = Do you **know how to** …? b) = Are you **allowed to** …? As a child I **was able to** skate all day. As a child I **could** skate all day. a) = it was **possible** (my feet didn't hurt/there was enough ice …) b) = I was **allowed** to	Die *present perfect*- und *future*-Formen von *can* werden mit *be able to* gebildet. **Beachte:** Da *can/could* mehrere Bedeutungen haben (vgl. § 1.1 – 1.10), wird *be able to* manchmal vorgezogen, um **Missverständnisse** zu vermeiden.

Prüfen Sie nun bitte nach, wie viel Sie gelernt haben.

6 Modals

Übungen

1
Make suggestions, using 'could'.

Example:
What shall we do tonight? (disco) –
We could go to the disco.

1. When shall we have our party? (next Saturday)
   We ...
2. What shall I give my mother for her birthday? (book)
   You ...
3. What shall we have for lunch? (some hamburgers)
   We ...

2
You want to be very polite. What would you say?

Example:
You have missed the school bus. Your sister has a bike.
...? (use)
Could I use your bike, please?

1. It is raining and you have to go out. Your father has an umbrella.
   ...? (borrow)
2. You want your brother to help you with your homework.
   ...? (help)
3. You want to know something from a neighbour.
   ...? (ask something)

3
What would you say in the following situations? Use the correct form of 'can' or 'be able to'.

1. You have just started a French course. You are going to France next year. What do you ask your teacher?
   ... I ... next year? (speak)
2. You are having a party, but there will be many more girls than boys. You tell your friend:
   You ... come if ... (bring) ... .
3. You want to buy a scooter, but you have to save enough money first.
   You think you will have the money next year.
   I think I ... next year. (buy)

Which rules helped you to choose the right modal?

4

Make the meanings of these sentences clearer by explaining them, using 'be able to' or 'be allowed to'.

1. James couldn't play football because he was ill.
   He ... play.
2. James couldn't play football because his father wouldn't let him.
   He ... play.

What could this sentence mean?

3. Can you come on holiday with us?
   a) ...
   b) ...

5

Translate the following sentences, using the correct form of 'can, could' or 'be able to'.

1. Kannst du Französisch?
2. Vor zehn Jahren konnte ich ganz gut Französisch.
3. Du könntest eine bessere Stelle finden, wenn du eine Fremdsprache lernen würdest.
4. Dürfte ich bitte dein Fahrrad ausleihen?
5. Leihst du mir dein Fahrrad?
6. Ich darf nicht ins Kino.
7. Ich kann nicht ins Kino, ich habe zu viele Hausaufgaben.
8. Maria kann bald Ski fahren, wenn sie ein bisschen übt.
9. Als Kind bin ich sehr schnell gelaufen.
10. Ich konnte noch nie Tischtennis spielen.
11. Darf ich Ihnen die Tasche abnehmen?
12. Das kann nicht die richtige Antwort sein.

Write down the number of the rule which helped you to find the correct answer.

6 Modals

Wissen

§ 2 Must – mustn't

	must		
§ 2.1	I really **must** stop smoking.	**Notwendigkeit.** (Siehe § 4.2)	
§ 2.2	Ties **must** be worn. You **must** work hard.	**Auffordern, zwingen, verpflichten.** *Must* ist eine sehr **starke Anweisung**. Der/die Angesprochene fühlt sich verpflichtet oder gezwungen. *Must* wird vornehmlich im formellen und geschriebenen Sprachgebrauch verwendet. (Siehe § 4.2)	
	You **needn't** wear a tie. (= Du **brauchst** keine Krawatte anzuziehen.) You **don't have to** work hard. (= Du **musst nicht / brauchst nicht** hart zu arbeiten.)	**Beachte:** Das Gegenteil von *must* ist nicht die Verneinung *must not*, sondern wird durch andere Hilfsverben wie *cannot, should not, need not, don't have to* usw. ausgedrückt.	
§ 2.3	The neighbours are very noisy. They **must be having** a party. I've seen Sue and Kevin together a lot. She **must** be his girlfriend.	**Logische Schlussfolgerung.**	
	So Jean **can't** be Kevin's girlfriend. (= Sie **kann nicht** seine Freundin sein.)	**Beachte:** Das Gegenteil von *must* wird nicht durch *must not* gebildet, sondern durch ein anderes Hilfsverb. That **mustn't** be = das **darf nicht** sein.	

	mustn't	
§ 2.4	You **mustn't** cross the road when the lights are at red. I **mustn't** forget to post Sue's letter. It's a secret. You **mustn't** tell anyone.	**Verbieten.** Eine sehr **starke Anweisung** bzw. **Verpflichtung**. *Mustn't* darf nicht mit „muss nicht" verwechselt werden: you **mustn't** = **du darfst nicht** du **musst nicht** = you **don't have to/ needn't** (Siehe § 4.2)

6
What do you think the headmaster is saying?
These words will help you:
It doesn't matter/I/wear.
Your son/wear/school uniform.

7
What must or mustn't you do when you see these signs?
Wherever possible write two sentences.

Tony …
… hamster

6 Modals

Übungen

8

What is the difference between the following statements?

a) She isn't Spanish, she's Italian.
b) She can't be Spanish, she must be Italian.

Rewrite these sentences, using 'must' to suggest that something is very probable or 'can't' if something is not probable.

Example:
The baby keeps crying. I'm sure she's hungry.
The baby **must be hungry**.

1. Kay is out all the time. It is obvious that she knows a lot of people.
   Kay ...
2. Bill is always borrowing money. I'm sure he doesn't earn very much.
   Bill ...
3. What! You're tired already. But you've only just got up.
   You ...
4. There's the doorbell. I'm certain it's the postman.
   It ...

§ 3 Must have

§ 3	David's late. He **must have** missed the bus. Look, Leslie is still waiting for her friend. She **must have been** standing there all afternoon.	**Logische Schlussfolgerung: Vergangenheit.**

Beachte:
In verneinten Sätzen verwendet man *can't have* (nicht *mustn't have*):
Kim passed me without speaking. She **can't have** seen me.

9

Complete these sentences by using 'must be -ing, must have, can have' or 'can't have'.

1. Look at this book on Sheila's desk, 'French in Ten Days'. She … French. (learn)
2. I haven't seen Mrs Bond for ages. I think she … away. (go)
3. I wonder where Joe has put that magazine. Surely he … it away? (throw)
4. I don't believe you. You … (joke)
5. Ring the bell again. I don't think she … you. (hear)
6. The light was on in the kitchen this morning. I … to switch it off last night. (forget)

6 Modals

§ 4 Have to – not have to

	have to	
§ 4.1	Sorry, I **have to** go now. Sorry, I**'ve got to** go now. Do you really **have to** go? **Have** you really **got to** go? Why did you **have to** go to the doctor's?	**Auffordern; Notwendigkeit** ausdrücken. **Beachte:** a) Zwischen *have to* und *have got to* gibt es keinen Bedeutungsunterschied. *Got* wird oft in der Umgangssprache vorgezogen, jedoch nur im *present tense*: **I've got to** go to the doctor's. **I had to** go to the doctor's yesterday.
	'How do I get a passport?' – 'You **have to** fill a form in.' (allgemeine Bestimmung) 'You**'ll have to** fill a form in.' (in deinem, Ihrem speziellen Fall)	b) **have to/will have to** Besonders in der gesprochenen Sprache wird *will have to* oft für spezifische Aufforderungen gebraucht, *have to* hat dagegen eine allgemeinere Bedeutung.
§ 4.2	'Do you really **have to** go now?' 'Yes, I **have to** go and see my grandmother.' (= „**Musst** du … gehen?" „Ja, ich **muss** …")	a) Vorsicht bei der Übersetzung von „müssen" im **Präsens**. *Must* wird nur für sehr starke Anweisungen und Verpflichtungen verwendet (vgl. § 2). *Have to* ist die **gängigere** Übersetzung.
	We **had to** wear ties to get into the disco. My brother's ill. We**'ve had to** call a doctor.	b) Die *past tense*-Formen von *must* werden mit *have to* gebildet.

	not have to	
§ 4.3	I **didn't have to** wait long at the doctor's. Mike **doesn't have to** go to work tomorrow. **Do** I **have to** go? You **don't have to** go.	**Keine Notwendigkeit.** Vgl. *need not* § 5. **Beachte:** **Frage- und Verneinungssätze** werden mit *to do* gebildet, im Gegensatz zu den anderen modalen Hilfsverben: **Can** I go?
	have to – must	
§ 4.4	What time do you **have to** get up tomorrow? I **must** get up early tomorrow. (= I think it's necessary) I **have to** get up early tomorrow. (= Someone or something else makes it necessary) Passengers **must** leave by the back door. Dogs **must** be kept on a lead.	**Auffordern; Notwendigkeit** ausdrücken. *Must* wird dann gebraucht, wenn die Aufforderung zur Handlung vom Sprecher selbst ausgeht. Dagegen drückt *have to* einen Zwang aus, der von anderen ausgeht. Für Fremdsprachenlerner genügt es zu wissen, dass *have to* in der **Umgangssprache** bevorzugt wird, *must* dagegen kommt eher im **offiziellen** und im **geschriebenen** Sprachgebrauch vor. Deutsche Sprecher neigen dazu, *must* viel zu häufig zu gebrauchen, das klingt aber für Briten sehr autoritär. Da *must* nur für sehr **eindringliche Aufforderungen** verwendet wird, ist es besser, in der **Umgangssprache have to** zu benutzen.

6 Modals

10

Complete these sentences by using 'must(n't)' or a form of 'have to'.

1. I'm sorry I couldn't come yesterday. I ... take my motor bike to the garage.
2. My sister ... to wear glasses since she was six.
3. You ... forget to give your father the message. It's very important.
4. ... you ... change trains last night?
5. Why ... Joan ... go to the doctor's yesterday? She cut her finger very badly.
6. ... Tony ... go to work by bus or can he walk it?
7. Why ... Dennis ... get up so early these days? He ... catch an earlier bus.
8. I can stay in bed tomorrow. I ... go to school.
9. Children under 14 ... be accompanied by an adult.
10. What ... I ... do to get a visa? ... I ... pay anything?
11. I can't stay any longer, I ... be home by eleven.
12. All passengers ... report to the information desk.

§ 5 Needn't/not have to – mustn't – needn't have – didn't need to

	needn't / not have to	
§ 5.1	You **needn't/don't need to/don't have to** come with me if you don't want. (= Du brauchst/musst nicht)	Etwas ist **nicht notwendig**. Zwischen *needn't, don't need to* und *don't have to* ist kein Bedeutungsunterschied.
	mustn't	
§ 5.2	You **mustn't** come with me. (= Du darfst nicht)	*Must not* darf nicht mit „muss nicht" verwechselt werden.
	needn't have – didn't need to	
§ 5.3	We **needn't have** booked seats. (= But we did) We **didn't need** to book seats. (= So we didn't)	Etwas **wäre nicht notwendig gewesen**: *needn't have*. Etwas **war nicht notwendig**: *didn't need to*.

6 Modals

Übungen

11
Explain the difference in each pair of sentences. Add something to each sentence to make the meaning clearer.

1. a) You mustn't shout at me.
   b) You needn't shout at me.
2. a) You mustn't tell Steve.
   b) You needn't tell Steve.

12
Rewrite these sentences so that they mean the same as the one above. Use 'not have to, needn't' or 'mustn't'.

Example:
I've already fed the cat. → You **needn't** feed the cat.

1. Don't eat all the biscuits.
   You … eat all the biscuits.
2. It is not necessary for you to get up early tomorrow.
   You … get up early tomorrow.
3. Wear a tie or not, just as you like. But no jeans.
   You …, but you … jeans.

13
In which of these sentences did the person actually walk / buy orange juice?

1. a) I needn't have walked all the way.
   b) I didn't need to walk all the way.
2. a) We didn't need to buy any orange juice.
   b) We needn't have bought any orange juice.

14
What did they say?

1. Valerie had no money, so she sold her stamp collection. A few days later she won a lot of money in a competition.
   'I … my stamps.'
2. Alan took his umbrella out with him, but it didn't rain.
   'I … my umbrella.'
3. Carol gave Mike a free ticket for a pop concert. The next day Mike told his mother:
   'It was free. I … pay.'

§ 6 May – might – may/might as well

	may	
§ 6.1	I **may** decide to leave school next year. You **may** be right. We **may not** be able to get tickets for tonight.	**Vermutungen; Möglichkeiten erwägen.** *May* darf nicht mit dem deutschen „mag" verwechselt werden: He **may** come = **Vielleicht** kommt er. (Nicht: er möchte kommen) **Beachte:** In **Fragen** wird *may* durch *can* oder eine andere Formulierung **ersetzt**: That **may** be true. **Can** that be true? **Is it possible that** it's true?
§ 6.2	**May** I have your attention, please?	**Erlaubnis erbitten.** Heutzutage klingt es **altmodisch und formell**, wenn *may* gebraucht wird, um Erlaubnis zu erbitten oder zu erteilen. *May* in dieser Funktion wird durch *can/could* ersetzt. *(Can/Could I use your phone? – Yes, you can.)*
	might	
§ 6.3	You **might** say you're sorry.	**Ärger** bekunden.
§ 6.4	I **might not** be able to come to the pop concert.	**Vermutungen, Möglichkeiten erwägen.**

6 Modals

	may – might	

§ 6.5	'Do you think Alan will come to the party?'
	a) He **may** do.
	   (neutrale Vermutung)
	b) He **might** do.
	   (stärkere Unsicherheit)
	
	My girlfriend **may** go to Scotland this summer.
	(50% Wahrscheinlichkeit)
	
	I **might** go with her.
	(30% Wahrscheinlichkeit)
		Der Bedeutungsunterschied zwischen *may* und *might* ist sehr gering.
		
		May drückt eine **größere Wahrscheinlichkeit** aus.

	may have – might have	
§ 6.6	I **may/might have** left my dictionary in the library. 'Julie's hair is wet.' – 'She **might have been swimming**.'	**Vermutungen über vergangenes Geschehen.** *May* drückt eine etwas größere Wahrscheinlichkeit aus, aber der Bedeutungsunterschied ist gering.
	may/might as well	
§ 6.7	There's nothing to do. We **may/might as well** go home. 'Shall we go out?' 'Why not? We **may/might as well**.'	Der Sprecher steht dem Vorschlag **gleichgültig** gegenüber.

15

Express these ideas in a different way, using 'can' or 'may/might'.

1. It is possible for me to leave school next year.
   I ...
2. It is possible that I will leave school next year.
   I ...
3. There is a chance that cigarettes will damage your health.
   Cigarettes ...
4. It has been found that cigarettes damage your health.
   Cigarettes ...

16

Sally hasn't arrived at school yet. What possible explanations can you think of? Use 'might (not), might (not) have' or 'might have been -ing'.

Example:
Perhaps she has missed the bus.
She might have missed the bus.

1. Perhaps she is not coming today.
   ...
2. Perhaps she is ill.
   ...
3. Perhaps she has gone to the doctor's.
   ...
4. Perhaps she didn't hear the alarm.
   ...
5. Perhaps she was dancing all night.
   ...

17

Rewrite these sentences, using 'might have, must have' or 'can't have'.

Sue knows our secret.
a) I'm sure Mike told her.   Mike ....
b) Perhaps Mike told her.   Mike ....
c) I know Mike hasn't talked to her yet. Mike ....

6 Modals

§ 7 Shall/should – should have – be to/be supposed to – ought to – had better

	shall	
§ 7.1	**Shall** I get you a cup of tea? Where **shall** we go? Who **shall** we invite to the party?	**Vorschläge, Angebote machen** oder **erbitten**.
	should	
§ 7.2	I think we **should** invite Ken to our party. He hasn't got many friends. What do you think I **should** do?	**Rat geben** oder **Vorschläge erbitten**. Im Gegensatz zu *shall* impliziert *should* eine **Verpflichtung**, z. B. moralischer, rechtlicher Art.
§ 7.3	You **should** enjoy the film. It's very funny. The meeting **shouldn't** go on for too long.	**Vermutungen:** etwas ist **wahrscheinlich**.
§ 7.4	'Go and get me a newspaper.' – 'Why **should** I?' 'Where's my purse?' – 'How **should** I know?'	**Ärger** bekunden.
§ 7.5	You **should be doing** your homework, not listening to music. You **shouldn't** speak to your parents like that.	**Raten, warnen, tadeln.** Vgl. *ought to* (§ 7.9).
§ 7.6	I **shouldn't** really be telling you this. (= But I am)	Die **Absicht, Verpflichtungen oder Ratschläge zu ignorieren**.
	should have	
§ 7.7	I **should have** worked harder, then I might have passed the exam.	**Verpflichtungen**, denen man **nicht nachgekommen** ist.

	be to/be supposed to	
§ 7.8	New pupils **are to** report to the headmistress at nine. 'Did you see the notice? We'**re supposed to** go and see Mrs Dean at nine.'	*Are to* und *be supposed to* drücken eine **Verpflichtung** aus, die z. B. durch eine **Regel** oder **Vereinbarung** festgelegt ist. *Are to* wird eher im **offiziellen** Sprachgebrauch verwendet, *be supposed to* ist **informeller**.
	ought to – ought to have	
§ 7.9	We **ought to** be very careful not to destroy the world we live in.	Vgl. § 7.5 Es ist kein großer Bedeutungsunterschied zwischen *should* und *ought to*. *Ought to* drückt eine **stärkere Verpflichtung** aus, z. B. moralischer oder rechtlicher Art.
§ 7.10	I **should** really do my homework, but I **ought to** help my mother. Our new neighbours don't know many people yet. Perhaps we **ought to have** invited them to our party.	Die Verpflichtung, der Mutter zu helfen, wird als stärker empfunden.
	had better	
§ 7.11	You **had ('d) better** hurry up. (= Or something unpleasant will happen) We'**d better not** go into that field. There's a bull in it.	**Raten, warnen, tadeln.** *Had better* drückt eine **stärkere Verpflichtung oder Warnung** aus als *should* oder *ought to*.

6 Modals   Übungen

18
Some of these signs tell you that you must or must not do certain things, others only suggest you should or should not do them. Put in 'must, mustn't, should' or 'shouldn't'.

You ... go jogging.

You ....

You ....

You ....

When there is a choice, for example if we can choose whether to go jogging or not, we use ... (should/must).

19
Translate the following sentences, using 'shall, should, ought to' or 'should have'.

1. „Diese Mathematikhausaufgaben sind sehr schwierig." „Soll ich dir helfen?"
2. Meine kleine Schwester hätte schon vor einer Stunde zu Hause sein sollen. Glaubst du, wir sollten die Polizei anrufen?
3. „Ich kenne eine sehr arme Familie." „Du solltest ihr etwas Geld geben!"
4. Eigentlich sollte ich meine Hausaufgaben machen, aber ich habe keine Lust dazu.
5. „Welche Telefonnummer hat Ken?" „Wie soll ich das wissen?"
6. Dieser Film müsste dich interessieren. Er ist über Großbritannien.
7. Die Leute sollten langsamer fahren.
8. Pass auf, dass du die Tasse nicht zerbrichst.

20
What did the lions say?
Use a form of 'should'.
"I suppose it would have been better if we hadn't done it."

I suppose ... really – they're terribly fattening.

§ 8 Will

	will	
§ 8.1	**Will** you come out with me on Saturday?	**Bitten.**
§ 8.2	'There's someone at the door.' – 'It **will be** the postman.'	**Vermutung**: etwas ist **sicher aufgrund** einer **logischen Schlussfolgerung**.
§ 8.3	I'**ll** help you. **Will** you have a cup of tea?	**Vorschläge, Angebote.**
§ 8.4	Tony **won't** help me, but maybe Sue **will**. My camera **won't** work	**Bestehende** oder **mangelnde Bereitschaft**. Im übertragenen Sinne auch für **Nichtbelebtes**.
§ 8.5	I **will** climb that mountain, just wait and see.	**Entschlossenheit.** In diesem Zusammenhang wird *will/ won't* in der gesprochenen Sprache **betont**.
§ 8.6	If you drop an egg it **will** break. Some people just **won't** stop worrying.	**Typische Verhaltensweisen** oder **Eigenschaften**.

Beachte:
Die Vergangenheitsform von *will* ist *would*:
I asked Carol if she **would** go out with me, but she refused.
Tony **wouldn't** help me last night.

6 Modals

21
Complete these sentences by using the correct form of 'will', 'won't' or 'would'.

1. 'We haven't got any bread.' 'I … go and get some.'
2. My CD player … work. Can you repair it?
3. … you baby-sit for me tonight?
4. … you baby-sit for me tonight, please?
5. We told Dave he should work harder for the exam, but he … listen. Now he's failed.
6. I … win this match if it's the last thing I do. I … lose again. (not/want)
7. My friend is a vegetarian. She … eat any meat at all.
8. 'The phone's ringing.' 'It … be Jean. She's gone away this weekend.'

§ 9 Want – would

	want	
§ 9.1	**Will** you come with me? (= eine Bitte) Do you **want to** come with me? (= Hast du Lust?)	*Will* darf nicht mit *want to* verwechselt werden.
	would	
§ 9.2	**Would** you help me with my homework, please?	**Höfliche Bitten.** Vgl. § 8.1. *Would* klingt höflicher und weniger aufdringlich als *will*.
§ 9.3	**Would** you like a cup of tea?	**Vorschläge, Angebote.** Vgl. § 8.3. *Would you like* klingt höflicher als *Do you want*.
§ 9.4	I**'d** like to go to England in the summer.	**Wünsche.**
§ 9.5	I**'d** rather go to Italy.	**Vorlieben.**
§ 9.6	A holiday in England **would** be nice.	**Sich etwas vorstellen.**

22
What does Andy's wife say? Use 'would' and 'might'.

[1] effort – the food I made for you; [2] tasty – good (tastes good)

7 Infinitive – ing-form

Haben Sie manchmal Schwierigkeiten mit Sätzen wie den folgenden? Wissen Sie oft nicht, ob man einen **Infinitiv** *mit to* oder *ohne to* gebraucht oder ob man eher die **ing-Form** verwendet?

> There's a lot of **work to be done**.
> Angela **wants me to marry** her.
> My parents won't **let me stay** out overnight.
> Linda waited **for** her boyfriend **to come**.
> A map is used **for finding** directions.
> I **remember buying** my first book.
> I **remembered to buy** the book.
> I watched Sue **mend** her bike.
> I watched Sue **mending** her bike

In diesem Kapitel finden Sie alles, was Sie wissen müssen, um den Infinitiv und die *ing*-Form richtig anwenden zu können.

Überprüfen Sie Ihr Wissen

1

Complete these sentences by using the correct form of the verb in brackets.

1. 'Have you finished … this book?' (read) 'Yes, do you want … it?' (borrow)
2. 'The doctor has advised me … so hard.' (not/work)
   'Why not … a holiday, then?' (take)
3. 'There's no point in … to the cinema now. (go) It's too late.'
   'Well, what about … television, then?' (watch)
4. That film is not worth … . (watch)
5. We've decided … to the pop concert, after all. (not/go)
6. Marion's parents won't let her … to the concert. (go)
7. After … for six months Christine has finally succeeded in … a job. (look, find)
8. I'm sorry about … the coffee on your shirt. (spill)
9. 'You don't look well. You'd better … at home today.' (stay)
   'No, I'd rather … to school. I'll be alright.' (go)
10. Brenda seems … on holiday. She's very brown. (be)
11. Sally doesn't like dogs. She is afraid of … . (bite)
12. 'Your hair needs … .' (cut) 'You know I can't stand … what to do.' (tell)
13. My friend is always trying to make me … new clothes. (buy)

2

Translate the following sentences into English.

1. Hast du dich schon entschieden, was du tun willst?
2. Hast du jemanden, mit dem du reden kannst?
3. Wenn du willst, dass ich dir helfe, musst du etwas warten.
4. „Wollen wir eine Tasse Tee trinken?" „Sehr gerne."
5. Wir warteten auf das, was kommen würde.

3

Can you explain the difference between these pairs of sentences?

1. a) Do you like to dance?
   b) Would you like to dance?
2. a) Can you remember giving Mike five pounds?
   b) Can you remember to give Mike five pounds?
3. a) Julie stopped talking to her friend.
   b) Julie stopped to talk to her friend.
4. a) We watched the zoo keeper feed the animals.
   b) We watched the zoo keeper feeding the animals.

7 Infinitive – ing-form — Wissen

§ 1 Der Infinitiv mit to

Der **Infinitiv mit *to*** steht in folgenden Konstruktionen:

§ 1.1		**Nach bestimmten Wörtern**:
	Brenda has **arranged to see** the manager about an interview. The job **seems to be** quite interesting.	a) Verben: *agree, appear, arrange, choose, decide, fail, help* (vgl. § 2.3), *learn, manage, offer, plan, promise, refuse, seem, tend, want* etc.
	There's a lot of **work to be done**.	b) Manchen Nomina
	The new boy in our class has **no-one to talk to**.	c) *Somebody, anything* …
	Show me **what to do**. Dave doesn't know **whether to leave** school or not.	d) Fragewörter/*whether*
	Sarah was the **first** girl **to win** a prize for science. She was **the only** person from our school **to get** a prize.	e) Ordinalzahlen/*the only*
	It's **too** late **to get** tickets now. Is it warm **enough to go out** without a coat?	f) *too/enough*
§ 1.2	My parents don't **allow me to smoke**. Sue **persuaded Jill not to give up** her job.	**Objekt + Infinitiv mit *to*** Nach Verben, die ein a) **Zulassen, Veranlassen** oder einen **Befehl** ausdrücken: *advise, allow, ask, expect, invite, order, persuade, remind, teach, tell, warn* etc.
	Linda's mother **wants her to marry** Trevor. Trevor **would like Linda to finish** her studies first.	b) **Wünschen, Wollen, Mögen** oder deren Gegenteil ausdrücken: *hate, hope, like, love, need, prefer, want, wish, would like/prefer* etc.

zu § 1.2		**Beachte:** Nach „wollen/mögen" steht im Deutschen ein Gliedsatz mit „dass". Dies verleitet zu dem Fehler, an *want* oder *would like* einen Gliedsatz mit *that* anzuschließen: ⊖ Linda's mother **wants that** she marries …
§ 1.3	**Would** you **like** to see my photos? **Do** you **want** to see my photos? (= Möchtest du meine Fotos sehen?) **Do** you **like** to see my photos? (= Siehst du sie gerne, normalerweise?) When Martin was young he **wanted** to be a train driver. Jean put her stamps away, but Steve **wanted** to look at them again.	**like/want** *Like* und *want* werden oft verwechselt. Vermeiden Sie die Vergangenheitsformen von *like* immer dann, wenn statt dessen *wanted* eingesetzt werden kann. **Nicht:** ⊖ … he **liked** to be a train driver. ⊖ … Steve **liked** to look at them again.
§ 1.4	Mike **wanted to go** to the concert, but it was so bad he **wished that** he hadn't gone.	**want/wish** *Want* kann **keinen irrealen Wunschsatz einleiten**. Statt dessen steht *wish that*.
§ 1.5	Ann waited **for her boyfriend to come** out of the shop. It's time **for me to go** to bed. It's unusual **for the weather to be** so bad in August.	**for + Objekt + Infinitiv mit *to***
§ 1.6	We stopped **to have** a drink. 'Do you want to come to town with me?' 'I'd love **to**.'	Der Infinitiv mit *to* drückt ein **Ziel** oder eine **Absicht** aus. **Beachte:** Um **Wiederholungen** zu vermeiden, steht oft *to* anstelle von *to* + Verb.

7 Infinitive – ing-form   Übungen

1

Translate the following sentences into English and write down the number of the rule which helped you. Always use infinitives.

1. Willst du mit mir tanzen? (höflich)
2. Ich habe Mike zum Tanzen aufgefordert, aber er wollte nicht. Ich wünschte, ich hätte ihn nie gefragt.
3. Meine Brieffreundin hat mich zu einem Ferienaufenthalt bei ihr eingeladen.
4. Werden deine Eltern die Kosten dafür übernehmen, dass du in den Ferien nach England gehst?
5. Die Lehrerin riet Thomas, nach Großbritannien zu gehen, um seine Englischkenntnisse aufzubessern.
6. Ist es für Ausländer leicht, in Großbritannien Ferienjobs zu bekommen?
7. Ich suche jemanden, der mir bei der Suche eines Ferienjobs hilft. Ich weiß nicht, wen ich fragen soll.
8. Es ist schwer für mich, mich auf englisch auszudrücken.
9. „Weißt du, wie man dieses Formular ausfüllt?" „Nein, und es ist niemand da, den man fragen könnte."
10. Kannst du warten, bis ich Geld gewechselt habe?
11. Susan wünschte, sie hätte John nicht zu ihrer Party eingeladen.
12. Willst du, dass ich früher komme?
13. „Will deine Schwester mitkommen?" „Sie möchte gern, aber das will ich nicht."

§ 2 Der Infinitiv ohne to

Der **Infinitiv ohne *to*** steht nach folgenden Verben bzw. Ausdrücken:

§ 2.1	Kate **made Tony help** her with the housework. Sue's parents **won't let her stay** out overnight.	**Veranlassen, erlauben:** **Make/let + Objekt + Infinitiv ohne to.**
§ 2.2	'It's late. We**'d better go** home.' 'I**'d rather stay** a bit longer.' **Why pay** more if you can buy it cheaper at this shop?	Nach *had better, would ('d) rather, why (not) …?*
§ 2.3	Will you **help me to mend** my bike? Will you **help me mend** my bike?	*help* + Infinitiv mit oder ohne *to*. Kein nennenswerter Bedeutungsunterschied.

Sind Sie sicher, wann man *to* vor den Infinitiv setzen muss und wann nicht? Prüfen Sie bitte nach.

7 Infinitive – ing-form   Übungen

2
Your British penfriend is staying with you. Compare the things you have to and don't have to do, at home and at school.

| My parents
Our teachers
I/We | (don't) | make me/us …
let me/us …
allow me to/us to …
have to … |

Write as many sentences as you can.

These words might help you: go to (parties …)/go to bed, get up early, at …/go out with …/stay out …/stay up late/in the week/at the week-end/bring friends home/do homework/two hours homework every day/speak English/be late/use biros/wear/smoke/ …

3
Finish each of these sentences so that it means the same as the one before.

Example:
1. a) Can I have your camera for a while?
      Can you **lend** me your camera for a while? (lend)

   b) I don't like the idea of lending you my camera.
      I … you my camera. (not want/lend)

2. a) We are going to meet at the town hall.
      We … at the town hall. (arrange/meet)

   b) Why don't you meet at the bus stop instead?
      Why not … at the bus stop instead? (meet)

3. a) We should get some more bread.
      We … some more bread. (had better/get)

   b) 'Will you get some more bread?' John asked Eric.
      John … some more bread. (ask/get)

4. a) What do you want to do, stay in or go out?
      … you … or …? (would rather/stay in/go out)

   b) I'd rather stay in.
      I've … . (decide/stay in)

§ 3 Die ing-Form (gerund)

Die **ing-Form** wird verwendet:

§ 3.1	Do you **enjoy reading** comics? I **don't mind not having** a television. I **can't stand being told** what to do.	Nach bestimmten **Verben**: *avoid, dislike, enjoy, feel like, finish, go/keep (on), give up, imagine, mind, miss, practise, stop, suggest, can't help/stand etc.*
§ 3.2	Have you ever thought **of working** abroad? Don't worry **about breaking** my CD. A map is used **for finding** directions. Gerald had danced **without stopping** for four hours. **After dancing** all night Trevor was very tired.	**Präpositionen + -ing**: *agree with, ask/talk about, believe in, think of, pay for, look forward to, keep on*, etc. *good at, happy/crazy/ disappointed/excited/worried about, tired/proud/afraid of, interested in, keen on, used to/for* etc. **Konjunktionen + -ing**: *after, although, before* etc.
§ 3.3	It's **no use/no good talking** to him. He doesn't listen. Diane **couldn't help laughing**. **What about/How about going** skating? It's **no fun walking** about in the rain. That film is**n't worth seeing**.	Nach bestimmten **Wendungen**: *it's no fun/good/use; it's (not) worth; can't help; what/how about …?/There's no point in …*
§ 3.4	Your hair **needs cutting**. This sweater **wants mending**.	**need/want + -ing**

7 Infinitive – ing-form   Übungen

4
Finish each of these sentences so that it means the same as the one before.

Example:
Which films do you like to watch? (enjoy)
Which films do you **enjoy watching?**

1. It will be nice to lie on the beach. (look forward to)
   I'm … on the beach.
2. It was strange for Thomas to drink tea with milk. (not used to)
   Thomas was … tea with milk.
3. Would you like to listen to a CD? (feel like)
   Do you … to a CD?
4. Can you take me to town please? (would mind)
   … you … me to town, please?
5. Neil hates to be alone. (can't stand)
   Neil … alone.
6. Carol is happy when she is alone. (enjoy)
   Carol … alone.

5
How does the woman explain what happened to the sweater she made?

'The cat … with the wool.'
(keep/play)

This cartoon is an example of rule § …

6

Complete the following sentences by using the -ing form, infinitive with 'to' or without 'to'.

1. I don't know your boyfriend, but I'd like ... him. (meet)
2. I'm looking forward to ... your boyfriend. (meet) Why not ... him round tonight? (bring)
3. My bike needs ... (mend), but I don't know when ... it. (do)
4. 'I'm tired of ... so hard. (work) I want ... (do) something different now.' 'What about ... a film, then?' (see)
5. The film was so sad it made me .... (cry)
6. Stop ..., will you? (cry)
7. 'What was the film about?' 'It's too difficult ... .' (explain)
8. Can you write a letter in English without ... a mistake? (make)
9. Barbara hasn't learned how ... her computer yet. (use)
10. Bob can't stand .... (be criticised)
11. 'There's no point in ..., let's go home.' (wait) 'I don't live far from here. It's not worth ... on a bus.' (get)
12. You should give up .... (smoke) The doctor has warned you .... (not/smoke)
13. It's no good ... about your exams. (worry) They're over now, so you'd better ... them. (forget)
14. 'I'm fed up with ... to school. (go) I'd rather ... a job.' (get) 'Why not ... school, then?' (leave)
15. 'What do you want to do after ... school?' (leave) 'I'd like ... abroad for a while.' (work)

Welche Sätze sind Beispiele für
(a) Regel § 3.1?
(b) Regel § 3.2?
(c) Regel § 3.3?
(d) Regel § 3.4?

7

Warum wird hier die ing-Form verwendet? Welche Regel gibt die Erklärung? § ...

... as I was saying, he's marvellous at carrying the shopping home, unless we meet a cat ...

7 Infinitive – ing-form

§ 4 Verben mit Infinitiv und ing-Form

Auf manche Verben kann sowohl der **Infinitiv** als auch die **ing-Form** folgen:

§ 4.1	We were just going out when it **started to rain/raining**. They **don't allow smoking** in this part of the cafe. They **don't allow you to smoke** in this part of the cafe.	Bei manchen Verben **verändert sich die Bedeutung kaum**, ganz gleich, ob dem Verb ein Infinitiv oder eine *ing*-Form folgt: *allow* (vgl. § 1.2a) *begin/start, continue, intend, like, love, hate, prefer*
	I **like getting up** early. (= ich mache es gern) I **like to get up** early. (= ich finde, das sollte ich tun)	**Beachte:** Wenn *like* „gern machen" bedeutet, gebraucht man eher die *ing*-Form. Wenn *like* bedeutet, dass man etwas **für richtig hält**, gebraucht man eher den **Infinitiv**.
§ 4.2		Bei anderen Verben **verändert sich die Bedeutung**, je nachdem, ob darauf ein Infinitiv oder eine *ing*-Form folgt:
	a) I still **remember/I'll never forget buying** my first book. I **remembered/didn't forget to buy** the book.	a) *remember/forget* + *ing*-Form: sich an etwas in der **Vergangenheit erinnern** *remember/not forget* + Infinitiv: sich erinnern, **etwas zu tun**
	b) Tony **stopped eating** his ice-cream. Tony **stopped to eat** his ice-cream.	b) *stop* + *ing*-Form: **aufhören**, etwas zu tun *stop* + Infinitiv: **aufhören, um** etwas zu tun
	c) 'I'm **trying to learn** Italian.' 'Have you **tried using** a CD player?'	c) *try* + Infinitiv: versuchen, ein **Ziel** zu erreichen *try* + *ing*-form: eine bestimmte **Methode** ausprobieren

§ 4.3		Verben der **Sinneswahrnehmung**: *see, watch, hear, listen to, feel, smell*
	I **watched** Sue **mend** her bike. It didn't take long.	Mit **Infinitiv**: ein Vorgang wird **insgesamt**, einschließlich seines Ergebnisses, erfasst.
	I **watched** Sue **mending** her bike for a few minutes, then I left.	Mit *ing*-**Form**: nur der **Teil** eines Vorgangs wird wahrgenommen, der sich gerade **im Ablauf** befindet, also noch nicht zu Ende ist.

7 Infinitive – ing-form

8

Derek's parents are away on holiday. They gave him a list of things to do while they were away. What has he remembered to do? What has he forgotten?

- take library books back
- collect coat from cleaner's
- water flowers
- post letters
- buy newspapers
- empty rubbish bin
- buy Jane's birthday present

1. He has ... (remember)
2. He has ... (forget)
   But his parents are not coming back until tomorrow, so he still has a little time. What does he say to himself?
3. I ... (must(n't) remember/forget)

9

You are sitting with an old friend remembering some of the things you once did together. Talk about your memories.

Example:
Do you remember **being bitten by that dog**? (bite/that dog)
I'll never forget **falling into the river**. (fall/river)

1. Do you remember ...?
   (go into hospital/you were ten; want to be a doctor)
2. I'll never forget ...
   (learn to ride a bike; go out with a girl/boy for the first time)
3. I'll always remember ...
   (cry on my first day at school; earn my first money)

Write down some of the things that you remember or will never forget.

10

Which of the forms in brackets completes the sentences?

1. 'I've tried … this maths homework, but I can't.' (to do/doing)
   'Have you tried … Jill? She's very good at maths.' (to ask/asking)
2. 'I can't go to sleep at nights.' 'Have you tried … a drink of warm milk before you go to bed?' (to have/having)
3. Sue is trying … enough money to buy a motor bike. (to save up/saving up)
4. 'My radio isn't working.' 'Why don't you try … a new battery in?' (to put/putting)
5. Barbara stopped … and stood up. (to talk/talking)
6. Barbara stopped … to her friend who had just got off the bus. (to talk/talking)
7. Shall we stop … something to eat? (to have/having)
8. If you don't stop … soon I'll go mad. (to sing/singing)

11

Think carefully about whether you need the infinitive or the ing-form in these sentences.

1. I heard Trevor … his guitar yesterday. (play) He played for me all afternoon.
2. I heard Trevor … his guitar yesterday. (play) Unfortunately I couldn't stay long.
3. Did you hear someone … as we passed that window? (sing)
4. I saw Manchester United … against Liverpool last week. (play) It was a great match from beginning to end.
5. The missing boys were last seen … near the old farm. (play) A woman saw them on her way home from work.
6. 'How do you know I came in late?' 'I heard you … up the stairs and go to the bathroom.' (come)
7. Diane watched the car … round the corner and drive away. (turn)
8. I saw Elizabeth … in the park as I went past on my bike. (sit)
9. I saw Elizabeth … down on a bench and start talking to a young boy. (sit)

Which rule helped you? § …

12

Can you work out what the first prisoner says?

'…'

(we're in time/being fed/them/I hope/to see)

8 Participles

Es gibt zwei Arten von Partizipien:

1. das **present participle**: *making, sitting*
2. das **past participle**: *finished, pleased*

Das **present participle** hat eine **aktive** Bedeutung:
The girl **telling** the story is a famous actress.
(= The girl is doing something)

Das **past participle** hat eine **passive** Bedeutung:
Did you hear the story **told** by that famous actress?
(= Something is done to the story)

Vergleichen Sie bitte die folgenden Sätze und überlegen Sie dabei, worin der Vorteil der Partizipialkonstruktionen besteht.

I know the girl who is playing table-tennis.	I know the **girl playing** table-tennis.
Jeff put down his book and looked at me in surprise.	**Putting down his book**, Jeff looked at me in surprise.
Frank fell asleep while he was watching the film.	Frank fell asleep **watching** the film.
Though she did not know what to expect, the detective pushed open the door.	**Though not knowing** what to expect, the detective pushed open the door.
Meat will go bad if it is not cooked immediately.	Meat will go bad **if not cooked** immediately.
Who's that boy who is standing near the door?	Who's that boy **standing** near the door?
There's a big car which is parked outside our house.	There's a big car **parked** outside our house.

Die Partizipialkonstruktionen sind kürzer und wirken geschliffener. Sie werden meistens im formellen, schriftlichen Sprachgebrauch eingesetzt. Es folgen einige weitere Beispiele für typische Partizipialsätze.

> **Not knowing** what to do, we went to the police station.
> Tony opened the door, **surprised** to see Jennifer.
> No wonder you've got a headache **with** your brother **making** so much noise.
> Although **done** by a child, the painting was extremely good.
> Children not **allowed** unless **accompanied** by an adult.
> Carol sat **reading** all afternoon.
> Why don't you **get** your hair **cut**?
> **Talking of** hair, have you **had** yours **dyed**?

8 Participles

Test

Überprüfen Sie Ihr Wissen

Translate these sentences into German.

1. Hearing the doorbell, Ann ran downstairs.
2. Jill cut her finger mending her bike.
3. Can you introduce me to the girl sitting near the window, please?
4. Four boys were sitting on the floor playing cards.
5. After being shown round Maria's new flat we all agreed that it was beautiful.
6. Are you going to have the flat wallpapered or do it yourself?
7. Kevin stood looking at the painting, absolutely fascinated.
8. Don't you think Diane looks better with her hair hanging down her back?
9. I've left my umbrella standing in the hall.
10. Having spent a sleepless night, we were all very tired.
11. Though paid very little, Eric is enjoying his new job.
12. Being unemployed, Jenny doesn't have much money.
13. With prices rising every day, I'm surprised people can still afford to buy cars.
14. Worried about the interview the next day, Cathy could not sleep.
15. Drivers must not stop on the motorway unless forced.
16. How would you like to spend a weekend at a luxury hotel, with all expenses paid?

§ 1 Partizipien anstelle adverbialer Gliedsätze

§ 1.1 Nebensätze der Zeit

Partizipien können Nebensätze der Zeit ersetzen. Sie werden oft durch *when, while, after, having* eingeleitet.

§ 1.1.1	**Walking** past Carol's house I saw her new bike in the garden. (= when I walked past …)	Wenn **zwei Handlungen gleichzeit**ig stattfinden, kann der **Temporalsatz** durch eine **Partizipialkonstruktion** ersetzt werden.
§ 1.1.2	Frank fell asleep (while) **watching** the film.	Läuft eine Handlung **gerade ab**, wenn eine **andere eintritt**, kann die Handlung, die **länger andauert**, durch eine *ing*-Form ersetzt werden.
	I hurt my foot (while) **jogging**.	Dabei kann *while* wegfallen, wenn dadurch keine Missverständnisse entstehen (vgl. § 1.4).
§ 1.1.3	**(After) having passed** the final exams, Sue started to look for a job. **After watching** the horror film Steve could not sleep. **Putting down** his book, Jeff looked at me in surprise.	Wenn eine Handlung **vor** einer anderen stattfindet, kann die **erste** durch eine Partizipialkonstruktion ausgedrückt werden.
§ 1.1.4	Susan waved to John **riding** past on a bike. a) **Susan** waved to John while **riding** past. (= Susan was riding) b) Susan waved to **John, who was riding** past. (= John was riding)	**Missverständnisse:** Manchmal muss die Partizipialkonstruktion durch *when* oder *while* eingeleitet werden, um klarzustellen, worauf sich der Partizipialsatz bezieht.

8 Participles

Wissen

§ 1.2 Andere Nebensätze: Grund, Begleitumstände, nach 'with', Einschränkung, Bedingung, Relativsätze

Ein Partizipialsatz kann auch andere Nebensätze ersetzen.

§ 1.2.1	**Not knowing** what to do, we went to the police station. **Having already seen** the film, I did not want to go again.	**Grund: Erklärungen** werden durch Partizipialkonstruktionen gebildet. Meistens stehen sie am **Satzanfang** und werden durch ein Komma getrennt.
§ 1.2.2	Tony opened the door, **surprised** and **pleased** to see Jennifer.	**Begleitumstände** werden oft durch Partizipien ausgedrückt (vgl. „indem, wobei"). Die *ing*-Form folgt oft nach Verben der Bewegung: *come, go, hurry, run, walk etc.*
§ 1.2.3	a) No wonder you've got a headache **with** your brother **making** so much noise. (= wenn Dein Bruder …) b) The best pupils in the school can go to America for a month **with** all expenses **paid**. (= wobei)	Partizipialsätze nach *with* sind in der Umgangssprache sehr häufig. Sie drücken oft Gründe (a) oder Begleitumstände (b) aus. Solche Konstruktionen werden oft mit „wenn, wobei (jedoch), da, und, während, jetzt/heutzutage wo, damals als" übersetzt.
§ 1.2.4	**Although done** by a child, the painting was extremely good. **Though not knowing** what to expect, the detective pushed open the door.	**Einschränkungen** können durch Partizipialsätze ausgedrückt werden. Sie werden durch *(al)though* eingeleitet.
§ 1.2.5	Meat will go bad **if not cooked** immediately. Children not allowed **unless accompanied** by an adult. (= if they are not with)	**Bedingungen** werden oft durch Partizipien ausgedrückt. Sie können mit *if* oder *unless* eingeleitet werden.
§ 1.2.6	Who's that boy **standing** near the door? There's a big car **parked** outside our house.	**Relativsätze** werden oft durch Partizipialsätze ersetzt.

1

Make one sentence out of two, using an ing-form.

Example:

Ken was sitting in the kitchen. He was talking to Jean.
Ken was sitting in the kitchen talking to Jean.

1. Alan was lying on his bed. He was listening to the radio.
2. Jeff broke his leg. He was skiing.
3. Sue heard the phone ring. She got up to answer it.
4. I got home. I was feeling tired.
5. I walked past the shop. I remembered I needed some milk.

In Satz 3 findet eine Handlung vor einer anderen statt. Woher wissen Sie, welche Handlung durch eine *ing*-Form ausgedrückt werden kann? Welche Regeln helfen Ihnen? Welche Regeln helfen Ihnen bei den anderen Sätzen?

2

Which words could you add to what this man is saying?

It IS me. I got the beard waiting out there for my flight.

3

Put brackets round the parts of the sentences which could be left out.

Example:

Have you seen a girl (who is) wearing a green coat?

1. My cousin lives in a house which was built a hundred years ago.
2. Everyone who is going on the coach trip should be here by seven.
3. The accident was seen by several people who were waiting at the bus stop.
4. Letters which are posted before six o'clock will be delivered the following day.

8 Participles Übungen

4
Can you describe these drawings? These words will help you: bear, bike, climb, giraffe, Mexican, ride, tree, walk, window.

  a … … ing a …

  a … … ing a …

  a … … ing … a …

Exercises 3 and 4 are examples of rule § …

5
Rewrite the underlined parts of these sentences using 'with' and a participle.

Example:
You can't go to school **if your head is aching like that.**
                     with your head aching like that.

1. I can't read the paper **if you interrupt me** all the time.
2. **Because travel is becoming cheaper** more and more people are going abroad for their holidays.
3. **Since there are only a few more minutes left** our team must try to score a goal.
4. There's a good bus service to town: **buses run every ten minutes.**

6
Translate the following sentences.

1. Having worked in America for two years, my sister has a lot of friends there.
2. Hearing a noise, Tony woke up.
3. Sue ran out of the house, banging the door after her.
4. I couldn't leave my brother alone yesterday with him feeling ill.
5. Can you smell something burning?
6. Cleaned and painted, that bike would look as good as new.
7. The dog came running up to us.
8. Being a foreigner, you need a visa to stay in this country.
9. Asked what she thought of the exam, Maria said it was too easy.
10. Though surprised, Carol said nothing.
11. Alan put the phone down, disappointed that Dave couldn't come.
12. This can will explode if left in a warm place.
13. The lake looks lovely with the sun shining on it.

8 Participles

Wissen   Übungen

§ 2 Partizipien nach bestimmten Verben

§ 2.1	Carol **sat reading** all afternoon. I've been **standing waiting** for you for ages.	Nach Zustandsverben wie *lie*, *sit*, *stand*, *stay* steht oft die *ing*-Form.
§ 2.2	Don't let me **catch** you **reading** my letters again. I'm sorry I **kept** you **waiting**. Why do you always **leave** your things **lying** about? Does your mother always **send** you **shopping**?	Nach *catch*, *keep*, *leave*, *send*.
§ 2.3	Why don't you **have/get** your hair **cut**? Eric has **had** his money **stolen**. (*get* würde heißen, er hat es absichtlich stehlen lassen!) I really must **get** my watch **repaired**. I really must **get** my homework **done**.	Nach *have/get* mit der Bedeutung „etwas machen/besorgen lassen". Der **Bedeutungsunterschied** zwischen *have* und *get something done* ist gering. *Have* bedeutet aber oft, dass etwas Unangenehmes passiert. *Get* deutet daraufhin, dass die Handlung etwas Mühe kostet. **Beachte:** *To get something done* kann auch bedeuten, dass man die Handlung selbst ausführt.

7

Ken is always complaining. Look at the things he keeps saying to his girlfriend.

Ken: – You always keep me …. (wait)
– You always leave the radio … even when you're not listening to it. (switch on)
– You keep … my library books. (read)
– I don't want to catch you … my comb again. (use)
– You sit … nothing all the time (do) and I've been standing … records in the shop all day. (sell)
– Why don't you get your hair … (cut)? It looks awful!

Ann: – Why don't you get yourself another girlfriend, Ken? Goodbye.

§ 3 Idiomatische Wendungen mit Partizipien

§ 3	**Considering** that Gordon has only been doing English for two years, he's very good. **Talking of** Jenny, I haven't seen her lately.	Partizipien in einigen Redewendungen: *considering, generally speaking, strictly speaking, judging from, seeing that, supposing, talking of, weather permitting, provided/providing that …* Solche partizipialen Wendungen werden durch Kommas abgetrennt.

8
Use each expression once to complete the sentences:
generally speaking, judging from, seeing that, supposing, weather permitting.

1. We'll have a picnic on Saturday …
2. … you won't be using your bike this afternoon, can I borrow it?
3. I don't … like westerns.
4. … they were to offer you the job, would you take it?
5. Linda's just had a shock … the look on her face.

9 If-clauses

Wozu brauchen wir *if*-Sätze?
Schauen Sie sich bitte die folgenden Beispiele an.

> If you lend me your skateboard you can borrow my bike.
> If you break my record you'll have to buy me another.
> I'll help you if you wait a minute.
> If our house were on fire I would call 999.
>
> Die Information, die uns am wichtigsten ist, steht am Satzanfang:
>
> Vgl. **You can borrow my bike** if you lend me your skateboard.

Man braucht *if*-Sätze immer dann, wenn Sachverhalte oder Ereignisse **von bestimmten Bedingungen abhängig** sind.

Solche Bedingungen können in drei Haupttypen eingeteilt werden:

> **A**: If I **do** A, then B **will/can/might/must/should happen**.
>   If A **happens**, then **do** B.
>
> **B**: If I **did** A, then B **would/could/might … happen**.
>
> **C**: If I **had done** A, then B **would/could/might … have happened**.

| Test | Wissen | Übungen | Lösungen | 9 |

Überprüfen Sie Ihr Wissen

1

Translate the following sentences into English.

1. Falls ich Zeit habe, helfe ich dir.
2. Wenn ich Zeit habe, helfe ich dir.
3. Wenn ich den Bus verpasse, nehme ich ein Taxi.
4. Ich gehe nicht zu deinen Freunden, es sei denn, man lädt mich ein.
5. Ich gehe auch dann nicht, wenn ich eingeladen werde.
6. Mein Vater redet mit mir, als ob ich ein Kind wäre.

2

In welchen der folgenden Sätze glaubt man, dass die Ereignisse im *if*-Satz (die Bedingungen) eintreten könnten? In welchen Sätzen ist man sich nicht so sicher?

1. If Brenda invites me to her party I'll go.
2. If Brenda invited me to her party I would go.
3. If the train arrives on time I'll be very surprised.
4. If the train arrived on time I would be very surprised.

3

Complete these sentences by using the correct forms of the words in brackets.

1. Will you write to me if I … you my address? (give)
2. Would you write to me if I … you my address? (give)
3. If Jill … her bike she won't get much for it. (sell)
4. If Jill … her bike she wouldn't get much for it. (sell)
5. If Jill for … her bike she wouldn't have got much it. (sell)
6. If they offered Sally the job … she … it? (take)
7. If they had offered Sally the job … she … it? (take)
8. Mike talks to Diane as if she … a child. (be)
9. If I only … Tina's address. (have)
10. I'll phone her when she … home. (get)
11. If the car … we would have gone on holiday last week. (not/break down)
12. If you … wear such long skirts you would look much better. (not/wear)
13. If we … to see old Mr Spinks he would be very pleased. (go) Shall we go tomorrow?
14. If Jane … to bed earlier last night she wouldn't be so tired today. (go)
15. If Kevin had worked harder he … the test. (might/pass)
16. What would you be doing now if we … to see you? (not/come)
17. If I … English better I would be very happy. (can/speak)

107

9 If-clauses

Wissen | **Übungen**

§ 1 If, when

Im Englischen gibt es zwei Wörter für das deutsche „wenn": *if, when(ever)*.

§ 1		
	If I have time I'll help you. **When** I have time I'll help you. **Whenever** I have time I'll help you.	Kann man „wenn" durch „falls" ersetzen, so benutzt man *if*. „**Falls** ich Zeit habe …" „**Wenn** ich Zeit habe …" „**Wann** immer ich Zeit habe …" Durch Umstellung des *if*-Satzes betont man eher den Hauptsatz: **I'll help you** if/when/whenever I have time.

Beachte:
Im Gegensatz zum Deutschen steht im Englischen **kein Komma vor dem if-Satz**.
I'll help you if I have time.

1

Translate these sentences into English, using 'if', 'when' or 'whenever'.

1. Wenn ich in die Stadt gehe, bringe ich dir eine Zeitschrift mit.
   a) (Marion ist sicher, dass sie hingeht)
      Marion: '… I go to town …'
   b) (Marion weiß nicht, ob sie hingeht)
      Marion: '… I go to town …'
2. Immer, wenn ich in die Stadt gehe, bringe ich meiner Mutter eine Zeitschrift mit.
3. Wenn ich älter bin, will ich Popstar werden.
4. Wir sind nicht sicher, ob wir nach Irland fahren. Aber wenn wir hinfahren, dann für drei Wochen.
5. Immer, wenn wir nach Irland fahren, besuchen wir meinen Brieffreund.
6. „Habe ich meinen Schlüssel bei dir liegen lassen, als ich heute morgen vorbeikam?" „Ich glaube nicht, aber wenn ich ihn finde, rufe ich dich an."
7. Immer, wenn ich Bilder von New York sehe, möchte ich hinfahren.
8. Was würdest du tun, wenn du von einem Hund gebissen würdest?
9. Was machen wir, wenn wir den Zug verpassen?

§ 2 If-Sätze vom Typ A: wahrscheinliche Bedingungen

Es ist nicht immer ganz einfach, nach *if* die richtige Zeitform des Verbs zu finden. Zunächst einige Regeln.

Typ A: If I **do** A, then B **will/can/might/must/should happen**.
If A **happens**, then **do** B.

§ 2.1	a) **If** you **don't hurry** you'll miss the bus. I can get a taxi **if** I **miss** the bus. **If** Ann **is** still in hospital we could go and see her. b) **If** Brian **is** still **having** a bath we'll have to go without him. **If** Sally **is feeling** sick she should go and lie down. c) **If** Tony **hasn't booked** his holiday yet he ought to hurry. If the train **has arrived** on time Aunt Mary will be here soon. d) **If** you **miss** the bus **get** a taxi. **If** Sally **is feeling** sick **tell** her to go and lie down.	Es werden Voraussetzungen oder Bedingungen genannt, unter denen etwas geschehen wird, kann, soll usw. Die Bedingungen werden für **erfüllbar** gehalten oder sind **bereits erfüllt** worden (reale Bedingungen): es ist noch möglich, sich zu beeilen, den Bus zu verpassen, dass sie im Krankenhaus ist usw. Je nachdem, ob sich die Bedingung auf ein **künftiges** Geschehen, ein Geschehen, das noch **im Verlauf** ist oder auf die **Vergangenheit** bezieht, steht im *if*-Satz das *simple present* (a), *present progressive* (b) oder das *present perfect* (c). Im Satztyp '*If A happens, then do B*' steht im Hauptsatz ein **Imperativ** (d).
§ 2.2	I won't go to the party **unless** I'm invited. (= if I'm not invited) I won't go **even if** I'm invited.	*Unless, even if:* Bedingungssätze können auch durch *unless* („wenn nicht") und *even if* („auch dann, wenn …") eingeleitet werden.

9 If-clauses — Wissen

§ 3 Will, should in Bedingungssätzen

§ 3.1		**will**
		Will wird in Bedingungssätzen **oft falsch** verwendet, z. B.: ⊖ If I **will miss** the bus I can get a taxi.
	If Joe **will talk/will insist on talking** all the time he'll soon have no friends. **If** Sally **will spend** so much money on clothes she'll soon have none left.	*Will* steht nach *if* nur mit folgender Bedeutung: – Jemand **will unbedingt** etwas tun oder nicht tun; jemand **pflegt**, etwas zu tun, häufig in Verbindung mit Verben wie *insist, refuse*.
	If you **will** wait here a moment I'll get the manager. **If** my father **will** lend me the car we'll go for a drive tonight.	– Jemand ist **willens** oder **bereit**, etwas zu tun. Diese Regeln treffen sowohl für reale als auch irreale Bedingungen zu. (Vgl. § 4.4 – 4.5)
§ 3.2	**If** there **should be** any problems let me know. (= but I don't expect any)	**should** Es wird für wenig wahrscheinlich gehalten, dass die Bedingungen erfüllt werden.
		Beachte: If there **are** any problems … (= there might be some)
	If I **shouldn't get** there on time don't wait for me. (= but I don't expect to be late)	**Beachte:** If I **don't get** there on time … (= I might not)
§ 3.3	**Should there** be any problems … **Should I** not get there on time …	*If* kann auch **weggelassen** werden. Dann muss aber *should* **vor dem Subjekt** stehen.

2

Put these two lists together and join them with the correct verb. At times you have to change the form of the verbs.

	~~too many sweets~~ — ask her to give me a ring.
	to read this book — we should win.
	Sally tonight — can watch the match on TV.
	smoking — look to the right first.
If you …	in our team — ~~you'll get fat~~
	home early we — come and see me.
	this form — I'll lend it to you.
	some free time — you'll be ill.
	a road in Britain — you can join the library.

Verbs: come, cross, <u>eat</u>, fill in, have, play, not give up, see, want

Example:
If you <u>eat</u> too many sweets you'll get fat.

3

Put the words in brackets into the correct tense.

1. Mike will soon have an accident if he … so fast. (drive)
2. Eric will never be ready on time if he … still … on the phone. (talk)
3. If the bus … soon I'll start walking. (not/come)
4. Julie won't give me my book back if I … her. (not/ask)
5. If you … a ticket for the play yet I don't think you'll get any one more. (not/buy)
6. If we … the play we'll leave before the end. (not/like)
7. If Jenny … to her CDs she won't hear us ringing the doorbell. (listen)
8. What! Linda is still in bed! I can't wait for her if she … yet. (not/get up). But if she … ready in ten minutes I'll give her a lift. (should/be)

9 If-clauses — Übungen

4
Complete these sentences with 'if', 'even if' or 'unless'.

1. I'll forgive you ... you say you're sorry.
2. You won't get a job ... you have good qualifications. They are absolutely necessary.
3. ... you have good qualifications it doesn't mean you will get a job.
4. Ring me ... you need help.
5. Don't ring me ... you need help. I'm very busy at the moment.
6. Ring me ... it's late at night. I don't mind.

5
Brian went to see his friend, Angela. But she was not in. Write out the message he left her.

> If you ___ to come to the match with me tomorrow let me know. Ring me ___ you get home. If I ___ not in I'll be at my mother's.

§ 4 If-Sätze vom Typ B: irreale Bedingungen

Typ B: If I **did** A, then B **would/could/might ... happen**.

§ 4.1	**If** Steve **passed** the exam he **could get** the job. (= but he probably won't)	Es ist **zweifelhaft**, ob die Bedingungen erfüllt werden (irreale Bedingungen).
§ 4.2	**If** I **had** the money I would buy a bike. (= but I don't have it) **If** I **were** you I would change my hairstyle. (= but I am not you) **If** our house **were/was** on fire I would call 999. **If only** I **knew** her phone number. He talks to me **as if** I **were** a child. She behaves **as if** she **owned** the place. **If only** he **wouldn't** talk to me as if I were a child. **If only** Ann **would** help me.	In Bezug auf die Gegenwart ist es **unmöglich**, dass die Bedingungen erfüllt werden (irreale Bedingungen). Bei *to be* wird in der Regel *I/he/she/it were* gebraucht, obwohl sich im gesprochenen Englischen *was* immer mehr durchsetzt. *If*-Sätze vom Typ B (und C) können auch durch *if only* und *as if* eingeleitet werden. Nach *if only* kann auch *would* folgen.
§ 4.3	**If** you **went** to see your grandmother she would be very pleased. (= Why not go and see her?) You might save enough money for a bike **if** you **got** a part-time job. (= Why not get a part-time job?) You could afford a bike **if** you **didn't spend** so much on clothes. (= Stop spending so much on clothes)	**Höfliche Vorschläge.** *If* + *simple past* hat keinen solchen starken Aufforderungscharakter wie *if* + *simple present*: **Beachte:** If you **go** to see your grandmother tomorrow she will be very pleased. You might ... if you **get** a part-time job. You will be able to afford ... if you **don't spend** ...

9 If-clauses — Wissen

§ 4.4	I would be grateful **if** you **would send** me/**could let** me have some information about hotels in Great Britain.	Für **formelle Bitten**, z. B. in offiziellen Briefen: *if + would/could*.
§ 4.5	**If** everyone **would give** just a little money we could help the poor. Jeff told Ann that **if** she **wouldn't help** him he wouldn't lend her any more books.	*If + would:* Wenn *would* nach *if* steht, drückt es meistens eine **Bereitschaft oder mangelnde Bereitschaft** aus.

6

Look at these pairs of sentences.

1. a) Would you go out with Ann if she asked you?
   b) Will you go out with Ann if she asks you?

2. a) Helen will go to America if she can save enough money.
   b) Helen would go to America if she could save enough money.

3. a) If Ken gets up early he won't be late for school
   b) If Ken got up early he wouldn't be late for school.

In welchen Sätzen glaubt man eher, dass die Ereignisse des *if*-Satzes eintreten könnten?

In welchen Sätzen ist man sich nicht so sicher?

7

Put the following two lists together.

If Joe passes the exam	she wouldn't be late.
If Joe passed the exam	we wouldn't be able to change money.
If the bank closes at three	we could have a picnic.
If the bank closed at three	his teachers will be very surprised.
If Harry gives Ann a lift	we won't be able to change money.
If Harry gave Ann a lift	we can have a picnic.
If the weather is fine	his teachers would be very surprised.
If the weather were fine	she won't be late.

9 If-clauses — Übungen

8
Look at this situation:

Diane thinks Carol should phone her brother, but Carol doesn't have his new phone number.

Carol says, **'I'd phone him if I had his new number.'** (phone/have)

Make similar sentences with 'if' + simple past.

1. Brian wants Eric to go to a football match with him, but Eric has to work.
   He says, '... .' (come/not have to)

2. Jill has seen a second-hand scooter that she would like to buy. But it is too expensive for her.
   She says '... so expensive.' (buy/not be)

3. Ann has been offered a job, but they don't want to pay her very much.
   She tells the manager, 'I ... if you ... more.' (take/pay)
   Then she goes home and tells her mother, 'If they ... I ... .' (give/take)

4. Derek is unhappy because he is so fat. But he eats a lot of cake. He says to his friend, 'If only I ... so fat.' (not/be)
   His friend answers, 'If you ... less cake you ... .' (eat/not be)

5. Mary is always tired. Steve thinks she goes to bed too late.
   He says, 'If you ... so late all the time you ... .' (not go to bed/not be)

§ 5 If-Sätze vom Typ C: nicht mehr erfüllbare Bedingungen

Typ C: If I **had done** A, then B **would/could** … **have happened**.

§ 5.1	a) **If** I **had known** you were ill I **would have come** to see you. '**If** the car **hadn't broken down** we **would have gone** on holiday yesterday.' 'Where **would** you have gone?'	Die Bedingungen sind **nicht erfüllt** und **können** auch **nicht mehr erfüllt werden**, weil sie sich auf die Vergangenheit beziehen. Sätze dieser Art dienen oft als **Erklärungen**.
	b) If Paul **hadn't drunk** so much last night he **wouldn't have** a headache now. 'What **would** you **be doing** now **if** I **hadn't come** to see you?' 'I**'d** probably **be watching** TV.'	Die Zeiten des Hauptsatzes ändern sich je nachdem, ob sie sich auf die Vergangenheit (a), Gegenwart (b) oder Zukunft (c) beziehen.
	c) **If** I **hadn't broken** my leg I **would go skiing** with you next week.	**Beachte:** *Would (have)* erscheint fast **nie** im *if*-Satz (vgl. § 4.4 und 4.5): If I **had known** you were ill … (**Nicht:** ⊖ If I **would have known** …).
§ 5.2	Ben walked past me **as if** he **had never seen** me before. **If only** I **hadn't taken** Sue's advice.	*If*-Sätze dieser Art können auch durch *as if* und *if only* eingeleitet werden.

Prüfen Sie nun bitte nach, ob Sie die verschiedenen *if*-Sätze richtig anwenden können.

9 If-clauses — Übungen

9

Look at this conversation:

'I wouldn't have done it like that.' (How ... you)
'How would you have done it, then?'

Make similar replies.

1. 'I wouldn't have paid as much as that.' (How much ... you)
2. 'You shouldn't have said that.' (What ... you)
3. 'I wouldn't have gone there.' (Where ... you)
4. 'You shouldn't have gone on a Saturday.' (When ... you)

10

Complete the sentences by using the information in the two lists.

Something happened	The effect
Joanne went to a party.	She was late for work this morning.
Barbara went outside with wet hair.	She caught a cold.
Frank lent Norman some money.	Norman could buy the bike.
Nobody told me Mr Jones was ill.	I didn't go to see him.
We brought a map.	We know where to go now.
Tony looked at a pretty girl.	He ran into a lorry.
Maria reminded Jeff about Ann's birthday.	He didn't forget it.
Sue didn't let Pete know she was coming.	He couldn't meet her at the station.
Caroline stayed up all night.	She is tired today.
Trevor lost his car keys.	We had to go by bus.
The Marsdens told us about this hotel.	We are staying here this week.
Derek didn't work hard.	He didn't pass the exam.

Example:
If Joanne hadn't gone to a party she wouldn't have been late for work this morning.

11

Which of these statements might have been made by
a) a good pupil before an exam?
b) a lazy pupil before an exam?
c) an ex-pupil?

1. 'If I worked harder I would probably pass.' …
2. 'If I had worked harder I would have passed.' …
3. 'If I work harder I should pass.' …
4. 'If only I had worked harder.' …

12

Which of these statements might have been made by
a) someone who is just learning to drive?
b) a bad driver?
c) someone who has just had an accident?

1. 'If I had driven more carefully I wouldn't have had an accident.'
2. 'If I drive carefully I won't have any accidents.'
3. 'If I were a better driver I wouldn't have so many accidents.'

13

Complete these sentences by using the correct forms of the verbs in brackets.

1. If the motor bike … so expensive Kate would buy it. (not/be)
2. If the bike … so expensive Kate would have bought it. (not/be)
3. You would be stupid if you … the job. (not/take) If I … you I would accept it. (be)
4. Debbie wouldn't go to New York even if she … the money. (have)
5. Debbie wouldn't have gone to New York even if she … the money. (have)
6. Alan would have been upset if we … him. (not/invite)
7. Alan will be upset if we … him. (not/invite)
8. Alan would be upset if we … him. (not/invite)
9. If Angela … her arm she would be playing in the team today. (not/break)
10. If Angela hadn't broken her arm she … last Saturday. (play)
11. If I … to drive a car I won't have to wait for buses all the time. (learn)
12. If I … a car I wouldn't have to wait for buses all the time. (can/drive)

10 Comparison of adjectives

Im Englischen gibt es viele Möglichkeiten, Vergleiche auszudrücken. Einige Beispiele:

> It's cheap**er** by bus.
> Cars are nois**ier than** bikes.
> I'm **the** old**est** in the class.
>
> Trains are **more expensive than** buses.
> That's **the most exciting** film I've ever seen.
>
> Your hands are **as** cold **as** ice.
> My English is getting **better and better**.
> **The longer** you stay up, **the more tired** you will be.

Prüfen Sie jetzt bitte nach, ob Sie diese verschiedenen Vergleichsformen richtig anwenden können.

Überprüfen Sie Ihr Wissen

1

Um Vergleiche auszudrücken, braucht man die Komparativ- und Superlativformen von Adjektiven. Kennen Sie diese Formen?

Nennen Sie die Komparativ- und Superlativformen von folgenden Adjektiven:

a) tall	e) big	i) short	m) easy
b) clever	f) simple	j) interesting	n) thin
c) bad	g) good	k) fat	o) modern
d) expensive	h) ill	l) much	p) many

Diese Adjektive sind Beispiele für drei verschiedene Steigerungsformen. Erkennen Sie die drei Gruppen?

War das schwierig? Wenn ja, sollten Sie sich § 1.1 und § 1.2 anschauen, bevor Sie weitermachen.

2

Complete each sentence so that it means the same as the one before.

1. No one I know is more intelligent than you. You are … person I know.
2. Riding a bike is not as difficult as driving a car.
   Driving a car is … riding a bike. (difficult)
3. A bike is not as fast as a car. Cars are … bikes.
4. Germany is warmer than Scotland. Scotland isn't … Germany.
5. These shoes are too small. I need a … size. (big)
6. You hardly ever write to me. Please write a bit … (often)
7. If you practise English more you will learn faster.
   … you practise … you will learn.
8. I prefer love stories to science fiction.
   Love stories are … science fiction. (good) They are … (romantic)
9. Finding a job is getting harder all the time.
   It's getting … and … to find a job.
10. No one has ever said such a nice thing to me.
    That's … thing anyone has ever said to me.
11. An increasing number of people are learning English.
    … and … people are learning English.
12. Health is important. So is money. Money is just … health.
13. I like it better here every day. … (long) I stay here … I like it.

10 Comparison of adjectives — Wissen

§ 1 Die regelmäßigen Steigerungsformen: Komparativ und Superlativ

§ 1.1	a) tall – taller – the tallest Let's go by bus. It's cheap**er**. I'm **the** old**est** in the class. b) simple – simpler – the simplest Which is easi**er**? English or Maths? I'm **the** cleverest person in our school.	Mit **-er, -est** gesteigert werden a) **einsilbige** Adjektive: *cheap, long, old, tall, short* etc. b) **zweisilbige** Adjektive, die auf **-er, -le, -ly, -ow, -y** enden: *clever, simple, lively, narrow, happy* **Beachte:** Im heutigen Englisch wächst die Tendenz, auch ein- und zweisilbige Adjektive in bestimmten Konstruktionen mit *more* zu steigern, z. B. *more cheap/clever than.*
§ 1.2	difficult – more difficult – the most difficult Geography is interesting. Music is **more interesting**. That's **the most exciting** film I've ever seen.	Mit *more* und *most* gesteigert werden **zwei- und mehrsilbige** Adjektive: *boring, expensive, fashionable, modern, private, serious, useful* etc.

§ 2 Die unregelmäßigen Steigerungsformen: Komparativ und Superlativ

| § 2 | I was **ill** yesterday, but today I'm much **better**.
That's the **worst** book I've ever read.
There aren't **many** sweets left.
Have you got any **more**? | Unregelmäßig gesteigert werden:
good, bad, ill, much, many, little.

good   better   best
bad
ill   worse   worst
much
many   more   most
little   less   least

Beachte:
Man fragt *Which do you like **best**?* auch dann, wenn es sich nur um zwei Sachen handelt. |

1
Complete this cartoon by using the superlative form of the opposite of 'heavy'.

I usually hold this one up for the proud father, it's the …

10 Comparison of adjectives   Wissen

§ 3 Vergleiche mit than, (not) as ... as, (bigg)er and (bigg)er, the (soon)er ... the (bett)er

§ 3.1	I'm tall**er than** you. It's cheap**er** by bus **than** by train. Trains are **more expensive than** buses.	Zum Ausdruck eines **höheren Grades**: -er than, more than
§ 3.2	Your hands are **as** cold **as** ice.	Zum Ausdruck des **gleichen Grades**: as ... as
§ 3.3	Your hair is**n't as** long **as** mine.	Zum Ausdruck eines **geringeren Grades**: not as ... as
§ 3.4	My English is getting bett**er and** bett**er**. The world is becoming a **more and more** dangerous place to live in.	Zum Ausdruck einer **stetigen Steigerung**: (bigg)er and (bigg)er, more and more (interesting) (immer interessanter)
§ 3.5	**The** soon**er** we get home **the** bett**er**. **The more** difficult a problem is, **the more** interesting it is. **The** long**er** you stay up, **the more** tired you will be.	Zum Ausdruck einer **proportionalen Steigerung**: the + -er/more ... the + -er/more ... (je ... desto ...).

2
Put the adjectives into the comparative form.

1. Can you come …? (early)
2. The … I get, the … I am. (old, happy)
3. I think you're … than the last time we met. (thin)
4. Can't you drive any …? (fast)
5. You're … at English than I am. (good)
6. English is getting … and … interesting for me. (much)
7. The … people who come on the trip, the … it will be. (many, cheap)

What is noisier than a jet?   ꜱʇǝɾ oʍ⟘

3
Use comparative or superlative forms of the adjectives in brackets.

1. … of the people in our class are older than me. (much)
2. 'Is your toothache better?' 'No, it's … .' (bad)
3. The … way to the station is through the park. (good)
4. If you need any … help give me a ring. (much)
5. That is the … mistake I have ever made. (bad)
6. Who is the … intelligent person you know? (much)
7. If you won't drive me home, the … you can do is lend me the bus fare. (little)

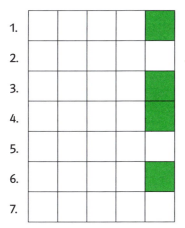

10 Comparison of adjectives   Übungen

4
Complete these sentences so that each one means the same as the one above it.

Example:
John's dog is seven. So is Tina's.
John's dog is as old as Tina's.

1. Linda is 1.75 m tall. Alan is 1.60 m.
   Linda is … Alan. (tall)
   Alan is … Linda. (short)

2. English is easy. So is Maths.
   English is just … Maths. (easy)

3. English is easy. Chemistry is more difficult.
   English is … chemistry. (difficult)
   Chemistry is … English. (difficult)

4. English is useful. Maths is useful, too.
   English is just … Maths. (useful)

5. Athens is about 27 °C in the summer, Madrid is about 25 °C.
   Madrid is … Athens. (hot)
   Athens is … Madrid. (hot)

6. About 3 million people live in Los Angeles; about 720,000 in San Francisco.
   Los Angeles is … San Francisco. (big)
   San Francisco is … Los Angeles. (big)
   There are … people in Los Angeles … in San Francisco. (more)
   There are … people in San Francisco … in Los Angeles. (many)

7. The Andes are 7,000 m high, the Rockies 4,500 m and the Atlas Mountains 4,000 m.
   The Andes are … . (high)
   The Rockies are … the Atlas Mountains. (high)
   The Atlas Mountains are … the Rockies. (high)

8. The red sweater costs five pounds, the green one five pounds fifty and the yellow one seven pounds.
   The yellow one is … . (expensive)
   The red one is … . (cheap)
   The green one is … the red one. (expensive)

9. Which is earlier: eleven thirty-two or twenty-seven minutes to twelve?
   … is … . (early)
   … is … . (later)

5
What do you think? Write down some of your opinions:

1. Boxing, ice-hockey, handball, basketball, football, motor cycle racing …
   exciting, interesting, dangerous, safe …
   more … than; the most …; not as … as …; just as … as …; etc.

Example:
Motor cycle racing is more dangerous than ice-hockey. Basketball is the most interesting. Motor cycle racing is not as exciting as basketball etc.

2. Westerns, love stories, thrillers, science fiction stories, war stories …
   exciting, interesting, relaxing, entertaining …

3. Collecting stamps, watching television, playing the (piano …),
   cooking, sewing, knitting, doing woodwork, reading, dancing …
   exciting, boring, restful, difficult, easy, interesting …

11 Adverbs

In diesem Kapitel wiederholen wir alles, was Sie wissen müssen, um die verschiedenen Adverbien richtig anwenden zu können.

Zunächst einige Beispiele:

Wir brauchen **Adverbien**, um Details anzugeben.
Sie beantworten die Fragen: **wann? wie? wie oft? wie lange?
bis zu welchem Grad? wo/wohin?**
Sie können auch Einstellungen und Kommentare des Sprechers ausdrücken.

> I got up **at seven o'clock**.
> The bus travelled **slowly**.
> Steve is **always** late.
> Carol stayed in England **for three weeks**.
> I was **very** nervous.
> Let's go **home**.

Prüfen Sie nun nach, wie viel Sie schon können.

| Test | Wissen | Übungen | Lösungen | 11 |

Überprüfen Sie Ihr Wissen

1

Complete the following sentences by changing the adjectives in brackets into adverbs.

1. It is … cold today. (awful)
2. Mrs Simmons is … ill. (critical)
3. It will … rain today. (probable)
4. Carol smiled at the new girl … . (friendly)
5. The old man climbed the stairs … . (difficult)
6. We got up very … this morning. (late)
7. Have you seen Helen …? (late)
8. 'Margaret has been working very … all week.' (hard)
   'That's … surprising, she's taking her exams next week.' (hard)
9. Your hair looks … . (nice)

2

Translate these sentences into English.

1. Es gibt einen Zug morgen Nachmittag um zehn vor fünf.
2. Gehst du noch in die Schule?
3. Sue hat noch keine Arbeitsstelle gefunden. Wahrscheinlich findet sie auch keine vor Weihnachten.
4. Wir gingen am Samstag in die Disco.
5. Mike spricht ganz gut Französisch. Angela auch.
6. Teresa steht immer früh auf.
7. Ich bin letzte Woche dreimal ins Kino gegangen.
8. Dieses Geschäft verkauft nur Hosen.
9. „Ich weiß nicht einmal Karins Telefonnummer." „Ich auch nicht."
10. Ich kann Ihnen leider nicht helfen. Ich bin nämlich fremd hier. Ich habe jedoch einen Stadtplan. Vielleicht hilft er Ihnen.

11 Adverbs — Wissen

§ 1 Arten der Adverbien

Man unterscheidet zwischen:

§ 1.1	I got up **at seven o'clock**.	Adverbien der **Zeit** *(adverbs of time)*: this morning, yesterday, at five o'clock, before lunch, for …, since … etc. (→ § 3)
§ 1.2	I caught the bus **round the corner**.	Adverbien des **Ortes**/der **Richtung** *(adverbs of place)*: at home, on the bus, under the table, outside, to school, into etc. (→ § 4)
§ 1.3	The bus travelled very **slowly**.	Adverbien der **Art und Weise** *(adverbs of manner)*: slowly, carefully, in a friendly way, with difficulty etc. (→ § 5)
§ 1.4	The journey **usually** takes twenty minutes.	**Häufigkeitsadverbien** *(adverbs of frequency)*: sometimes, often, always, usually, never etc. (→ § 6)
§ 1.5	I was **very** nervous when I finally arrived for the interview.	Adverbien des **Grades** *(adverbs of degree)*: very, completely, fairly, quite, pretty, too, enough, almost, a bit etc. (→ § 7)
§ 1.6	'I **only** had a sandwich for lunch.' 'I didn't have much **either**.'	**Hervorhebende** Adverbien *(focusing adverbs)*: also, even, only, especially, mainly, either … or, neither … nor etc. (→ § 8)
§ 1.7	**Luckily**, my new boss was a very understanding woman.	**Satzadverbien** *(sentence adverbs)*: naturally, luckily, unfortunately, maybe, anyway etc. (→ § 9)

§ 2 Die Bildung von Adverbien

Anders als im Deutschen unterscheiden sich die meisten englischen Adverbien von Adjektiven der Form nach:

Adjektiv   **Adverb**
a slow car   he drove slow**ly**

Es gibt einige Regeln, die man bei der Bildung von englischen Adverbien beachten muss:

§ 2.1	intelligent – intelligent**ly** clear – clear**ly**	**Die meisten Adverbien** werden **von Adjektiven abgeleitet**, indem man *-ly* anfügt.
§ 2.2	What a **lovely** dress! She is very **friendly**.	Vorsicht bei **Adjektiven**, die **auf -*ly* enden**! An diese Adjektive wird **kein *-ly*** angehängt. Sie werden oft mit *way* **umschrieben**: *in a lively, silly, friendly way.*
§ 2.3	I got up **early**. (adv.) I took an **early** train. (adj.) I work **hard**. (adv.) This chair is **hard**. (adj.) You speak English **well**. (adv.: „gut") I am not very **well**. (adj.: „gesund")	a) Einige Adverbien haben die gleiche Form wie das entsprechende Adjektiv: *fast, high, low, deep, near, far, late, long, daily, weekly, early, hard.* b) Einige Adverbien und Adjektive haben bei **gleicher Form verschiedene Bedeutungen**.
§ 2.4	Susan works **hard**. Susan **hardly** works. The plane is flying **high**. This book is **highly** interesting. **Adjektiv** **Adverb** hard (= hart) hard (= hart) hardly (= kaum) high (= hoch) highly (= sehr) short (= kurz) shortly (= bald) near (= nah) nearly (= beinahe) late (= spät) lately (= vor kurzem)	Manche Adverbien haben eine **andere Bedeutung als die Adjektive**, von denen sie ursprünglich abgeleitet wurden.

11 Adverbs

§ 2.5	These shoes feel comfortable. (= **are** comfortable) This tastes awful. (= **is** awful) The answer is correct.	Nach den Verben *be, look, feel, seem, smell, sound, taste* steht, da es sich ja nicht um eine Tätigkeit handelt, ein **Adjektiv**. **Beachte:** She looked serious. (Adj.: Sie sah ernst aus.) She looked at me seriously. (Adv.: Sie sah mich ernst an.) I feel **good**. (Adj.: wohl) I feel **well**. (Adj.: gesund)

1

Complete these sentences by forming adverbs from the adjectives in brackets.

1. The film will … be over before eleven. (probable)
2. 'Do you think we'll be able to get tickets?' '… .' (hopeful)
3. Neil looks very … today. (cheerful) He is smiling … to himself. (happy)
4. Alan plays the guitar very … . (good)
5. Jill couldn't stay …, she was in a hurry. (long)
6. That woman must be … rich. Have you ever seen her car? (fantastic)
7. The magazine 'Lifestyle' appears … . (weekly)
8. You are … right. (absolute)
9. 'If we set off … we'll get there on time.' (early)
   'Yes, but don't drive too … .' (fast)
10. Carol smiled at the new girl … . (friendly)
11. Grandfather climbed the stairs … . (difficult)
12. 'What are you cooking? It smells … .' (good)
    'Yes, it tastes quite … too.' (nice)

2

Translate these sentences into English.

1. Martin Luther King kämpfte hart für die Rechte der Schwarzen.
2. Kannst du etwas lauter reden, bitte. Ich kann dich kaum hören.
3. Helen wohnt in der Nähe vom Bahnhof.
4. Gestern habe ich beinahe meinen Bus verpasst.
5. Dieser Turm ist sehr hoch.
6. Dieses Buch ist höchst interessant.
7. Heute Abend komme ich spät nach Hause.
8. Hast du Barbara in letzter Zeit gesehen?

Which rule helped you? § …

11 Adverbs   Wissen

§ 3 Adverbien der Zeit (adverbs of time)

Diese Adverbien beantworten die Frage **„wann?"**, **„(für) wie lange?"**, **„wie oft?"**.
Sie stehen:

§ 3.1	We're going to a disco **tomorrow night**. Don't do that **again**. Carol stayed in England **for three weeks**.	Meistens am **Satzende**, besonders: *again, late, now, these days, then, today, this (morning), yesterday (afternoon), two months ago, for …, since …* etc.
§ 3.2	We're going to have a lot of fun today: **first** we'll go to the fair, **then** we'll see a film and **afterwards** we'll go to a party.	Am **Anfang** eines Satzes oder Nebensatzes, wenn sie **hervorgehoben** werden **oder** zur **Gegenüberstellung**, besonders: *afterwards, earlier, eventually, finally, first, immediately, lately, next, once, soon.*
§ 3.3	Tony has to be home **by ten on weekdays**. I was born **at midnight on New Year's Day in 1990**.	Bei **mehreren adverbialen Bestimmungen** ist die Reihenfolge: **genauere Angabe + weniger genaue** *at midnight – on New Year's Day – in 1990*

§ 3.4		*Still:* etwas **dauert länger als erwartet** (noch immer). *Still* steht
	a) I **still love** you. b) Jill **is still** in bed. c) Do you **still collect** stamps?	bei **bejahten** Sätzen und **Fragen**: a) *still* + Verb b) *be* + *still* c) hat das Verb mehrere Teile, so bleibt die Reihenfolge: *still* + Vollverb
	d) The letter **has still not** come.	bei **verneinten** Sätzen: d) Hilfsverb + *still* + *not* Um *still* hervorzuheben, kann man die Reihenfolge ändern:
	e) The letter **still has not** come.	e) *still* + Hilfsverb + *not*
§ 3.5	Is Sandra back **yet**? Sandra isn't back **yet**.	*Yet:* Erkundigungen, **ob etwas eingetreten** ist (schon) und **verneinten Antworten** darauf (noch nicht). Stellung: **Satzende**. **Beachte:** Is Sandra back **already**? (= Verwunderung ausdrücken)

11 Adverbs — Übungen

3
Put these sentences in the correct order and say which rules helped you.

1. on Fridays/doesn't close/the shop/until eight
   The shop ...

2. by about eleven/home/should be/we
   We ...

3. on Saturday nights/go out/I/with my friends.
   I/on Sundays/but/with my parents/go out
   I ...
   ... with my parents.

4. in August/going/on holiday/we're.
   to see me/my penfriend/is coming/in September
   We're ... to see me.

5. open/still/the shop/is
   The shop ...

6. I/to school/go/still
   ...

7. haven't met/yet/my penfriend/I
   I ...

8. play/you/still/the guitar/do/?
   ... the guitar?

§ 4 Adverbien des Ortes/der Richtung (adverbs of place)

Diese Adverbien beantworten die Fragen „**wo?**" und „**wohin?**". Sie stehen:

§ 4.1	Can you meet me **at the station**? Mary wants to visit a friend **in hospital**. It's cold **outside**.	Am **Satzende**.
§ 4.2	**At the station** there was a huge crowd of people. **Here** comes the bride. **There**'s Dennis. I wonder where he's going.	Am **Satzanfang**, wenn sie besonders **hervorgehoben** werden. *Here* und *there* stehen oft am **Anfang**.
§ 4.3		Treffen **mehrere Adverbien zusammen**, gilt folgende Reihenfolge:
	a) The town hall is **in the Market Square in the town centre**.	a) **genauere Angabe + weniger genaue**
	b) We went **to the cinema last night**. Let's go **home early**. We'll meet **at the bus stop tonight**. I have been going **to school for ten years**.	b) **Ort/Richtung + Zeit** O(rt) vor Z(eit) im Alphabet
	c) We'll meet **tonight at the bus stop opposite our house**. We'll meet **in town at the pub near the town hall**.	c) **kurz + lang**

11 Adverbs   Übungen

4
Der Mann am Fenster sagt auf Deutsch:
„Das da drüben ist das Empire State Building."
What is he saying in English?

5
Translate these sentences into English and say which rule helped you.

1. Meine Großeltern wohnen in einem kleinen Haus auf dem Lande.
2. Ich wurde 1986 in einem kleinen Dorf im Süden geboren.
3. In Deutschland trinkt man viel Kaffee. In Großbritannien trinkt man mehr Tee.
4. Wir fahren im Juli nach Frankreich.
5. Der Zug kommt um sieben Uhr achtundvierzig in Paris an.

6
Neil had a busy time last week. Write down all the things he did.
Start each sentence with 'He …'.

MON	
TUES	have lunch with Eve (town)
WED	afternoon – watch football match at Alan's
THURS	evening – night school
FRI	evening – take Julie to cinema
SAT	morning – play table-tennis at youth club
SUN	

§ 5 Adverbien der Art und Weise (adverbs of manner)

Diese Adverbien beantworten die Frage **„wie?"** (auf welche Art und Weise?).

Sie stehen:

§ 5.1	You speak English very **well**. Dora opened the letter **slowly**.	Normalerweise am **Satzende**.
§ 5.2	Dora **slowly** opened the letter.	Zur **Hervorhebung** werden manche Adverbien, z. B. *quickly, slowly, carefully,* **vor das Verb** gestellt. **Beachte:** Im Gegensatz zum Deutschen erscheint das Adverb im Englischen nicht zwischen Verb und Objekt: Dora öffnete **langsam** den Brief.
§ 5.3	**Suddenly** there was a crash. **Luckily**, no one was hurt.	Um eine **dramatische Wirkung** zu erzielen, werden manche Adverbien an den **Satzanfang** gestellt. (Vgl. § 9).
§ 5.4	Steven read the article **carefully** and **with great interest**. Mrs Davies sat **quietly in her armchair every evening**. **Every evening** Mrs Davies sat **quietly in her armchair**.	Treffen **mehrere** Adverbien **zusammen**, gilt folgende Reihenfolge: a) **zwei Adverbien der Art u. Weise kurz + lang** b) **Art u. Weise + Ort/Richtung + Zeit** A vor O vor Z Um eine **Anhäufung** zu **vermeiden**, wird die **Zeitbestimmung** oft an den **Satzanfang** gestellt.

11 Adverbs

§ 6 Adverbien der Häufigkeit (adverbs of frequency)

Diese Adverbien geben darüber Auskunft, **wie oft** und **ob überhaupt** etwas passiert bzw. passiert ist.

§ 6.1	Steve **is always** late.	*Be* + Adverb.
§ 6.2	Steve **always comes** late. Alan has **never danced** with a girl. Have you **ever driven** a car?	**Adverb + Vollverb.** In dieser Stellung stehen meistens *always, often, usually, sometimes, never*. **Beachte:** Im Deutschen ist die Reihenfolge umgekehrt: Steve **kommt immer** zu spät.
	I **usually have to** wait for Steve.	**Beachte:** *Have to* wird als Teil des Vollverbs angesehen, deshalb steht die adverbiale Bestimmung vor *have to*.
§ 6.3	**Never** drink when you're driving. **Usually** I get up early, **but** today I was late.	Wenn das Adverb besonders **hervorgehoben** werden soll, steht es am **Anfang** des Satzes (oft in Verbindung mit *but* oder *(al)though*.
§ 6.4	We have English **three times a week**. I have only met Derek **once**.	Einige Häufigkeitsadverbien stehen normalerweise am **Satzende**: *once, again and again, a few times, now and then, now and again, (twice) a (day)*.
§ 6.5	Marion went **to London twice**. Marion went **to London twice last year**.	Treffen **mehrere** Adverbien zusammen, so gilt folgende Reihenfolge: a) **Ort/Richtung + Häufigkeit** b) **Ort/Richtung + Häufigkeit + Zeit**

§ 7 Adverbien des Grades (adverbs of degree)

Diese Adverbien beantworten die Frage „**bis zu welchem Grad?**". Sie dienen auch zur **Verstärkung** einer Aussage.

§ 7.1	Brian is **very** ill. I **completely** forgot to post your letter. It's **quite a** long way. I **quite** like this CD.	**Vor** dem **Wort**, das sie näher bestimmen: *quite, very, really, completely, hardly, almost, a bit, too, enough* **Beachte:** *quite* steht **vor** *a(n)*
§ 7.2	I don't **really think** so. It will **probably rain** tomorrow. Jeff **probably won't** come.	Bei **Verben mit mehreren Teilen** *(don't … think, will … rain).* Adverb + Vollverb **Beachte:** In **verneinten** Sätzen steht *probably* **vor dem Hilfsverb**.
§ 7.3	Turn the radio down **a bit**, please. I don't like that music **much**.	**Much, a lot, a bit, a little** stehen am **Satzende**, wenn sie ein **Verb** näher bestimmen.

11 Adverbs

7
Translate these sentences into English.

1. Deine Mutter spielt erstaunlich gut Tischtennis.
2. Jennifer zeigte uns stolz ihre Briefmarkensammlung.
3. Der Sportlehrer erklärte sorgfältig die Spielregeln.
4. Janet zog schnell ihren Mantel an und eilte aus dem Haus.
5. Unser Nachbar kickte wütend unseren Ball aus seinem Garten.

Auf welche Regel muss man besonders achten?

Im Englischen darf das Adverb … zwischen … und … stehen (§ …).

8
Answer these questions about yourself, using 'I always/sometimes/usually, never …'.

1. When do you go to bed on weekdays?
2. When do you get up in the week?
3. What do you do in the evenings on weekdays?
4. What do you do on Saturday nights?
5. Is there anything you never do?

Which rule helped you? § …

9
Make complete sentences, using the adverb in brackets. Write down the rule which helped you.

1. The Donalds/have lived/in the country   (always)
2. We/have sports   (once a week)
3. Susan/has been/to a pop concert   (never)
4. Derek/has been out/with Linda   (a few times)
5. I/have to/tell my parents/where I'm going   (always)
6. I/can remember/that girl's name   (never)

10

Choose a word from each box to complete these sentences. Only use each word once. Always start with the first box.

awfully	probably	seriously
completely	quite	terribly
nearly	quite a	very
probably	really	

be	ill	nice
changed	interesting	sorry
cheap	know	won't be able
hot	missed	

Example:
It's **awfully hot** in here. Can we open a window?

1. Brian's mother is … in hospital.
2. Don … the train, he got up so late.
3. I'm … I broke your sunglasses.
4. These CDs are … . They're less than a pound.
5. I … to go on holiday this year. I haven't enough money.
6. When Sally went back to the village where she was born everything had … . She hardly recognised it.
7. Diane is … person. She's … to talk to.
8. 'What time are you coming home?' 'I don't … but I'll … late.'

11 Adverbs

§ 8 Hervorhebende Adverbien (focusing adverbs)

Diese Adverbien **heben** einen Teil des Satzes **hervor**.

§ 8.1	I like sports, **especially football**. I **especially like** swimming. Diane goes swimming and she **also plays** hockey.	Meistens **vor dem Ausdruck**, den sie näher bestimmen, besonders: *also, especially, even, just, mainly, mostly, only*.
§ 8.2	We **are just** good friends.	*Be* + Adverb.
§ 8.3	I don't **particularly like** swimming. Eric can't **even boil** an egg.	Bei Verben mit **mehreren Teilen: Adverb + Vollverb**.
§ 8.4	'I like classical music.' – 'I do, **too**. But I like pop **as well**.' 'I don't like classical music and I don't like pop **either**.' 'Andy doesn't like **either** pop **or** classical music.' – 'Well, I don't **either**.'	*Too, as well, either* stehen am **Satzende**.
§ 8.5	**Neither** of the films looks particularly interesting: **neither** the western **nor** the love story.	*Neither … nor* stehen immer am **Anfang**.

Das war doch ganz einfach, oder nicht? Mal sehen …

11
Translate these sentences into English.

1. Ich gehe nur einkaufen. Ich komme gleich wieder.
2. Wir sind nur eine Stunde im Konzert geblieben. Wir konnten nicht einmal Sitzplätze bekommen.
3. Sue liest Comics. Sie liest aber auch Zeitungen.
4. John kann am Wochenende nicht kommen. Mike kann auch nicht.
5. „Ich habe meine Hausaufgaben noch nicht gemacht." „Ich auch nicht."

§ 9 Satzadverbien (sentence adverbs)

Diese Adverbien beziehen sich auf den ganzen Satz. Sie **drücken eine Einstellung oder einen Kommentar des Sprechers aus**.

§ 9.1	**Honestly**, I don't care what people think of me. **Obviously**, you don't believe me.	**Normalerweise** am **Anfang**: *actually, anyway, hopefully, however, in fact, officially, maybe, of course, obviously, perhaps, surely, (un)fortunately, from (my/a) … point of view.*
§ 9.2	Bill has to go into hospital, **unfortunately**. The operation, **however**, will not be a difficult one.	**Manchmal** am **Satzende**. **Beachte:** *However* steht oft in der **Satzmitte** und wird durch Kommas als Kommentar gekennzeichnet.

12

Translate the following sentences into English. Use adverbs to express the highlighted words, but be careful where you put them.

1. Ich kann euch **leider** nicht am Bahnhof abholen.
2. Es gibt hier **bestimmt** eine Bank in der Nähe.
3. **Hoffentlich** kann ich im Sommer nach England.
4. Ob ich die Stelle bekomme, hängt **natürlich** von meinen Prüfungsergebnissen ab.
5. Hast du **übrigens** Tony in letzter Zeit gesehen?
6. Sylvia hat **vielleicht** recht.
7. **Im Grunde** stimme ich Ihnen zu. Es gibt jedoch eine Schwierigkeit.
8. Der Unfall war **glücklicherweise** nicht so schlimm.
9. „Sollen wir zu dem Fußballspiel gehen?" – „Mir gefällt Fußball **eigentlich** gar nicht. **Um ehrlich zu sein**, ich hasse es." – „Ich **persönlich** habe auch kein großes Interesse an Fußball."

11 Adverbs

§ 10 Inversion

Manchmal wird eine adverbiale Bestimmung besonders hervorgehoben, um eine dramatische Wirkung zu erzielen.

§ 10	**Never had I** seen such a crowd. **Not only did he** take us all out, he also paid for the meal. **Under no circumstances are you** to leave this room.	**Hervorhebung des Adverbs** (meistens nur in der **geschriebenen** Sprache) macht eine **Inversion von Subjekt und Hilfsverb notwendig**, vgl. die normale Stellung: **I had never** seen such a crowd. Adverbien, die eine solche Inversion notwendig machen: *not only, hardly, no sooner … than, never, not until, under no circumstances, only.*

13

Rewrite the following by putting the highlighted adverbs at the beginning of the sentence and making the necessary changes.

1. We had **hardly** gone to bed when there was a knock at the door.
2. Peter had **no sooner** arrived than he had to go again.
3. Doreen can **not only** play the piano, she is also a well-known folk singer.

14

Rewrite the sentences with highlighted words in them, following rule § 10.

Mr and Mrs Gambols' niece and nephew have come to stay with them for a few days. But **the children had no sooner** arrived than they started running round the living-room. The boy fell down and put his foot through the television. **He not only** broke the set, but also his leg and arm and he hurt his head. Mrs Gambol had to fetch the doctor.
The doctor had hardly left when the little girl kicked a football through the window. **She not only** broke the window, she als cut her arm on some glass. It was **not until** the children were in bed that **the Gambols could** sit down and rest. "George," said Mrs Gambol, "**you're** not to invite those children again, **under no circumstances**."

§ 11 Englische Verben anstelle deutscher Adverbien

Viele deutsche Adverbien werden im Englischen nicht durch Adverbien, sondern durch Verben wiedergegeben.

Beispiele:
It's **getting** cold. = Es wird **allmählich** kalt.
Anne **tends to** make careless mistakes. = Anne macht **gerne** Leichtsinnsfehler.

§ 11	Deutsche Adverbien	Englische Verben
	andauernd	go on/keep on
	anscheinend	appear/seem
	allmählich	get/grow
	bekanntlich	as everyone knows
	früher	used to
	gern	tend to; like; prefer
	leider	be afraid/sorry
	lieber	prefer
	nämlich	you know/you see
	offenbar	appear/seem
	sicher	be sure/certain
	vielleicht	may/might
	vermutlich	suppose
	weiter(hin)	go on/keep on
	zufällig	happen to

15
Translate the following into English.

1. Lach' nicht andauernd.
2. Andy hat anscheinend eine neue Stelle.
3. Früher habe ich gerne Briefmarken gesammelt.
4. Heute mache ich lieber Sport in meiner Freizeit.
5. Tony hat die Fahrprüfung nicht bestanden, aber er sagt, er versuche es weiter. Vielleicht hat er das nächste Mal Glück.
6. Dieser Film wird allmählich langweilig.
7. Ich kann am Samstag leider nicht kommen.
8. Bist du sicher, dass der Zug um zehn ankommt? – Ja, aber er hat offenbar Verspätung.
9. Haben Sie zufällig einen Stadtplan von London?
10. Es ist vermutlich billiger mit der Bahn zu fahren. Ich habe nämlich nicht viel Geld.

12 Indirect speech

Es gibt zwei Möglichkeiten, das, was man selbst oder was ein anderer gesagt hat, wiederzugeben:

a) durch Wiederholen der wörtlichen Rede, z. B.:
   'Don't drive too fast!'
   Sue **said**, 'Don't drive too fast.'
b) durch **indirekte Rede**. Hier hat man verschiedene Möglichkeiten, sich auszudrücken.

direct speech	indirect/reported speech
Ann: 'I **know** what to do.'	Ann **said**, '**I know** what to do.' Ann **says** she **knows** what to do. Ann **said** she **knows** what to do. Ann **said** she **knew** what to do.
Derek: 'I **went** to the cinema **last night**.'	Derek **told** me he **went** to the cinema **last night**. Derek **told** me he **went/(had gone)** to the cinema **the night before/on Monday**.
Neil: '**I** bought **this** sweater for **my** girlfriend.'	Neil **showed me a sweater** and **told** me he had bought **it** for **his** girlfriend.

Überprüfen Sie Ihr Wissen

Complete these sentences.

1. Joe: 'I'm not coming to the party on Saturday.'
   Joe says he … coming to the party on Saturday.

2. Mike: 'What were you doing when I phoned?'
   Mike wanted to know what I … when he phoned.

3. Grandma: 'If I had known you were coming I would have made a cake.'
   Grandma said that if she … we were coming she … a cake.

4. Eric: 'If I knew Tony's number we could ring him.'
   Eric said that if he … Tony's number we could ring him.

5. Sue: 'I want to learn to drive.'
   a) Sue told me she … to learn to drive. She's having her first lesson next week.
   b) Sue told me she … to learn to drive, but I think she has changed her mind now.

6. Sue: 'I like Mike.'
   Sue told me that she … Mike.

7. Jill: 'I don't smoke.'
   Ben: 'Look, Jill's smoking! She told me that she … smoke.'

8. Jill: 'I had a bad dream last night.'
   a) Jill told me she … a bad dream last night.
   b) Jill told me she … a bad dream the night before.

9. Jeff: 'I don't know if I can help you.'
   a) Jeff said he didn't know if he … help us.
   b) Jeff said he didn't know if he … help us.

10. Neil: 'I bought this sweater for my girlfriend.'
    Neil told me he had bought … sweater for his girlfriend.

11. On Friday Chris says: 'It's my birthday tomorrow.'
    Last Friday Chris told me that it was his birthday … .

12. Diane: 'What shall I do?'
    Diane didn't know … .

12 Indirect speech — Wissen

§ 1 Die Funktionen der indirekten Rede

Die indirekte Rede kann für folgende Zwecke gebraucht werden:

§ 1.1	Sue: 'Don't drive too fast!' – Sue **told** me not to/**said** I shouldn't drive too fast. Prime Minister: 'That's nonsense'. – The Prime Minister **did not accept** the suggestion.	Für **neutrale, distanzierte** Berichte. Die Aussage wird berichtet, **ohne** sich mit ihr zu **identifizieren**: man gibt **keine Gewähr für die Richtigkeit**; man gibt auch nicht zu erkennen, wie man selber dazu steht.
§ 1.2	Linda to Ann: 'Switch that radio off.' – Linda **politely asked/begged/ ordered/warned** Ann to switch her radio off. Sue: 'Don't drive too fast.' – Sue **warned/advised** me not to drive too fast. Prime Minister: 'That's absolute rubbish!' – The Prime Minister **disapproved of/ completely rejected/laughed at** the suggestion.	**Detailliertere** bzw. **subjektivere** Berichte. Der Berichterstatter muss auch die **Art** und den **Ton** der wörtlichen Rede wiedergeben, z. B. ob es sich um eine höfliche Bitte, einen Befehl, einen Ratschlag, eine Empfindung, Hoffnung, Befürchtung usw. handelt. Dabei kann die Aussage natürlich absichtlich gefärbt werden. Häufige Verben: *advise, ask politely, complain, criticise, doubt, hope, order, promise, suggest, warn* usw.
§ 1.3	Ken: 'I**'ll lend** you £5.' – Dave: 'Ken **said** he **would lend** me £5, but he hasn't done yet.'	Die indirekte Rede wird oft gebraucht, um auf **Fehlinformationen, Widersprüche** und **nicht eingehaltene Versprechen** hinzuweisen (§ 4.3).

1

Report the following statements

a) without adding your own opinion
b) with your own opinion added.

Use the following words: *say, tell, warn, order, shout (to), advise, promise, finally allow, complain.*

Example:
Keith to Ann: 'Don't drive so fast!'

a) Keith **told** Ann not to drive so fast.
b) Keith **warned/advised** Ann not to drive so fast.

1. Mike to Steve: 'I'll help you.'
   a) Mike … he would … .
   b) Mike … to help Steve.

2. Mr Reed to Ben: 'Get out of my garden!'
   a) Mr Reed … to get … .
   b) Mr Reed … to get … .

3. Frank: 'It's cold!'
   a) Frank … was cold.
   b) Frank … that … was cold.

4. Mrs Williams to her daughter: 'Don't go out without a coat.'
   a) Mrs Williams … not to go … .
   b) Mrs Williams … not to go … .

5. Mr Jennings to Sarah: 'Alright, you can go to the pop concert.'
   a) … that Sarah could … .
   b) … Sarah to go … .

Bei der Wiedergabe von wörtlicher Rede muss man manchmal einige Veränderungen vornehmen, manchmal nicht.

12 Indirect speech

Wissen Übungen

§ 2 Einleitendes Verb im present tense, present perfect, future: keine Veränderung der direkten Rede

| § 2 | Joe: 'I've failed my exam.'

a) – Joe <u>says</u> he **has failed** his exam.
– Listen. Joe is <u>telling</u> Sue that he **has failed** his exam.
b) – <u>Has</u> Joe <u>told</u> you that he **has failed** his exam?
c) – Joe <u>won't</u> tell anyone that he **has failed** his exam.
– Joe <u>will have told</u> his girlfriend that he **has failed** his exam. | Wenn das einleitende Verb im
a) *present tense*
b) *present perfect*
c) *future*
steht, bleibt die **Zeit der direkten Rede unverändert**. |

2
Write out these messages in full, then tell your friend what they mean.

Example:
Uncle George's telegram: ARRIVING SATURDAY
George: 'I'm arriving on Saturday.'
You to friend: Uncle George says he's arriving on Saturday.

1. Steve's telegram: LOST PASSPORT
Steve: 'I've ... .'
You to friend: Steve says he ... .

2. Mary's telegram: MONEY STOLEN
Mary: 'My ... has ... .'
You to friend: Mary says her ... .

3. Martin's note: Going to cinema tonight. Go with me?
Martin: 'I ... tonight. Do you want ...?'
You to friend: Martin says ... tonight.
He asks if we ... him.

4. Derek's note: Rang you yesterday. Weren't in. Call in tonight.
Derek: 'I ... you yesterday, but ... .'
'I'll ... .'
You to friend: Derek says ... me yesterday, but ... . He says he ... .

§ 3 Einleitendes Verb im simple past oder past progressive: keine Veränderung der direkten Rede

§ 3.1	a) Mike: 'What **were** you **doing** when I phoned?' – Mike wanted to know what I **was doing** when he phoned. (Unusual 'had been doing') b) Frank: 'I **had not seen** mountains before I went to Austria.' – Frank said **he had not** seen mountains before he went to Austria. c) Grandma: 'If I **had known** you were coming I **would have made** a cake.' – Grandma explained that if she **had known** we were coming she **would have made** a cake.	In folgenden Fällen bleibt die **Zeit der direkten Rede unverändert**: Die **wörtliche Rede** steht im a) *past progressive* b) *past perfect* c) *If*-Satz, Typ C (Das *past progressive* kann zu *past perfect progressive* verändert werden; das ist aber **höchst selten**).
§ 3.2	Eric: '**If** I **knew** Tony's phone number we could ring him.' – Eric said that if he **knew** Tony's number we could ring him. Carol: 'I **wish** the exams **were** over.' – Carol said she wished the exams **were** over.	Das *simple past* in **irrealen Bedingungs- und Wunschsätzen** wird beim Berichten **nicht verändert**.

12 Indirect speech   Wissen

§ 3.3	Mr Thatcher: 'I **was involved** in the deal … I **met** my mother … .' – Mr Thatcher admitted (…) that he **was involved** in the 1981 deal and **met** his mother during her official visit to Oman. *(Observer, 15. 2. 84)*	Das *simple past* der wörtlichen Rede bleibt **häufig unverändert**, besonders dann, wenn der in der wörtlichen Rede ausgedrückte Zustand bzw. Vorgang **nicht so lange her** ist.
§ 3.4	a) Sue: 'I **want** to learn to drive.' ↳ Sue told me she **wants** to learn to drive. (= she still wants to) Vgl.: Sue told me she **wanted** to learn to drive. (= I don't know if she still wants to) b) Jean: 'My boyfriend is **working** in York.' ↳ Jean told me that her boyfriend **is working** in York. (= he still is) ('… **was working** …') (= I don't know if he still is) c) Eric: 'Carol **has bought** a moped.' ↳ Eric was telling me that Carol **has bought** a moped. (= I believe him) '… **had bought** …' (= I'm not sure if that is true) d) Ann: 'Jeff **is having** a party tonight!' ↳ Ann said that Jeff **is having** a party. (= I believe he will) … **was having** … (= I'm not sure if he really will)	In den folgenden Fällen kann, muss sich aber nichts ändern. Die **wörtliche Rede** steht im a) *simple present* b) *present progressive* c) *present perfect* d) *future* Die Zeiten **bleiben erhalten**, wenn die **Aussage** zum Zeitpunkt des Berichtens **noch zutrifft** bzw. **bevorsteht**. (Vgl. § 4.1) **Beachte:** Wenn die oben genannten Zeiten bei der Wiedergabe in der indirekten Rede **verändert** werden, bedeutet es meistens, dass der Berichtende an der Aussage **zweifelt**. (Vgl. § 4.3)

§ 3.5	Sue: 'I **like** Mike.' – Sue told me that she **likes/liked** Mike. My penfriend: '**Is** Alan British?' – My penfriend wanted to know if you **are/were** British.	Für **Allgemeingültiges** kann sowohl das *simple present* als auch das *simple past* gebraucht werden. Es besteht kaum ein Bedeutungsunterschied.

Das sieht zunächst vielleicht etwas verwirrend aus. Aber nur keine Angst!
Die Übungen helfen Ihnen, Fehler zu vermeiden.

12 Indirect speech — Übungen

3

Complete these sentences by reporting what someone else said. Write down the numbers of the rules which helped you.

1. Brenda: 'Sometimes I wish I had a part-time job.'
   Brenda told me that she sometimes wishes she … a part-time job.
2. Elaine: 'I was listening to the radio this afternoon, so I didn't hear the phone.'
   Elaine explained that she didn't hear the phone because she … to the radio.
3. Tony: 'I'd send a telegram if I were you.'
   Tony remarked that he … send a telegram if he … me.
4. Mike: 'I think Dennis will help us.'
   Mike thinks that Dennis … help us. Shall we ask him?
5. Carol: 'I think Eric would help, too. Let's ask him.'
   Carol thought that Eric … too. She suggested that we should ask him.
6. Maria: 'Dennis could have helped us last night. He would have had time. He just didn't want to.'
   Maria believed that Dennis … us last night. She thought he … time, but that he just …to.

4

Look at these pairs of sentences.

1. a) Janet said you **are** very nice.
   b) Janet said you **were** very nice.

Bei welchem Satz würden Sie sich mehr freuen? Warum?

2. a) Dennis asked if we **were** looking forward to our holiday.
   b) Dennis asked if we **are** looking forward to our holiday.

Bei welchem Satz weiß man, dass der Urlaub noch bevorsteht?
Bei welchem Satz ist es nicht klar, ob der Urlaub schon vorbei ist?

3. a) Mike told me he **loves** Angela.
   b) Mike told me he **loved** Angela.

Bei welchem Satz würde sich Angela eher freuen? Warum?

4. a) Marion told me she **was** moving to Sheffield.
   b) Marion told me she **is** moving to Sheffield.

Bei welchem Satz ist man nicht sicher, ob sie noch umziehen will?

§ 4 Einleitendes Verb im simple past oder past progressive: Veränderungen in der direkten Rede

§ 4.1	Mary: 'I **want** to go home.' – Mary said she **wanted** to go home, but no-one listened. – Mary said she **wants** to go home. I'll go with her. Dave: 'My bike**'s been stolen**.' – Dave told me his bike **had been** stolen. (He didn't know that his brother had borrowed it.) – Dave told me his bike **has been** stolen. (He's going to tell the police.) Tony: 'I**'ll** see you on Christmas Eve.' – Tony told me he **would** see me on Christmas Eve.	Die Zeiten **ändern** sich wie folgt, wenn die **Handlung** oder das **Geschehen** der **direkten Rede vergangen** ist und **keine Auswirkung auf die Gegenwart** hat. (Siehe auch § 3.2–4; § 4.2). **wörtliche Rede** **indirekte Rede** simple present → simple past pres. progressive → past progr. present perfect → past perfect will-future → would am going to → was going to is leaving → was leaving future perfect → future in (will have) the past (would have)
§ 4.2	Jill: 'I **had** a bad dream last night.' ① Jill was saying she **had** a bad dream last night. (Bericht noch am selben Tag.) ② Jill was saying she **had/had had** a bad dream the night before. (Bericht einige Tage später.)	Wenn die wörtliche Rede im *simple past* steht, kann das *simple past* bei der Wiedergabe in der indirekten Rede zu *past perfect* verändert werden. Es **unterbleibt aber immer häufiger**, besonders dann, wenn der in der wörtlichen Rede ausgedrückte Zustand bzw. Vorgang nicht so lange her ist (vgl. § 3.4).

12 Indirect speech   Wissen   Übungen

| § 4.3 | a) Jill: 'I **don't smoke**.'
– Ben: 'I <u>thought</u> you **didn't smoke**.'
(= but now you are smoking)

b) Sue: 'I**'m doing** my homework.'
– Mother: You <u>told</u> me you **were doing** your homework, but you're listening to the radio!

c) Derek: 'I**'ve** just **done** the shopping.'
– Father: I <u>thought</u> Derek **had done** the shopping. But we've no eggs and I can't see any butter!

d) Lynne: 'I**'m coming** tomorrow.'
– Mike: You <u>said</u> you **were coming** tomorrow. Why have you changed your mind? | Um auf **Widersprüche, Fehlinformation** und **nicht eingehaltene Versprechen** hinzuweisen, werden *simple present* (a), *present progressive* (b), *present perfect* (c) und *future* (d) bei der Wiedergabe **geändert** (vgl. § 3.4).

Beachte:
'You said you **don't smoke**.'
(= I suppose that is still true.) |

5
Think carefully about these sentences before completing them, using the verbs in brackets.

1. Linda: 'I'm taking a computer course.'
   Linda told me that   a) she … a computer course. She seems to like it.
   (take)   b) she … a computer course. But that was several months ago. She might be doing something different now.

2. Wendy: 'I'll be very busy next week.'
   Wendy warned me that   a) she … very busy the following week.
   (be)   b) she … very busy next week.

3. Ken: 'I saw Sue at a party a few nights ago.'
   Ken told me that   a) he … Sue a few nights ago.
   (see)   b) he … Sue a few nights before.

§ 5 Die modalen Hilfsverben in der indirekten Rede, einleitendes Verb im past tense

§ 5.1	Jeff: 'I **can't** come tonight.' – Jeff said he **can't** come tonight.	a) Die **modalen Hilfsverben bleiben bestehen**, wenn die Aussage zum Zeitpunkt des Berichtens **noch zutrifft bzw. bevorsteht**.
	Steve: 'The TV **won't** work.' – Steve said the TV **won't** work. (= it still won't) Steve said the TV **wouldn't** work. (= but now it's alright)	b) Wenn aber der **Zeit- und Situationsbezug** der wörtlichen Rede **ein anderer** ist, so werden die Hilfsverben wie folgt **geändert**: can → could shall → should may → might will → would
§ 5.2	'All the windows are closed. Ted **must be** out.' – We decided that Ted **must be** out because all the windows were closed.	a) *Must* zum Ausdruck einer Annahme: Bleibt in der indirekten Rede **unverändert**.
	The doctor told my father that he **must** stop smoking. Ten years ago the doctor told my father that he **had to** stop smoking. So he did.	b) **Verpflichtung**, eines **Zwanges**: Wenn die Notwendigkeit immer noch besteht, bleibt *must/have to* erhalten. Besteht die Notwendigkeit nicht mehr, so wird sie durch *had to, would have to, should* ersetzt.
	Mother: 'You **needn't come** with me if you don't want to.'	Diese Regel gilt auch für *need*:
	Mother said I **needn't go** with her.	Die Situation der direkten Rede besteht noch.
	Mother said I **didn't have to** go with her.	Der Zeitbezug der indirekten Rede ist ein anderer.

12 Indirect speech

Übungen

6

Complete these sentences by choosing the correct verb from the box.
Which rules helped you to choose?

might	should	should have
must	mustn't	should

1. 'You should wear a tie tonight.'
   a) My girlfriend thought I … wear a tie tonight.
      Are you going to wear one?
   b) My girlfriend thought I … worn a tie tonight.
      Everyone else did.

2. 'I may be late, so don't wait for me.'
   Derek warned us that he … be late, so we didn't wait for him.

3. 'You mustn't forget to send me a postcard.'
   a) Martin said we … forget to send him a postcard when we go on holiday.
   b) Martin said we … send him a postcard, but we forgot.

7

I'd like to introduce the friends
you said I could invite for lunch.

What do you think the little boy's mother said?

This cartoon is an example of rule § …

12 Indirect speech — Wissen

§ 6 Veränderungen bei Pronomina, Zeit- und Ortsangaben, Fragen

§ 6.1	Martin: 'Do **you** like **my** new hairstyle?' – Martin asked **me** if **I** like/liked **his** new hairstyle.	**Personal-** und **Possessivpronomina** müssen an die veränderte Situation des Berichts angepasst werden.
§ 6.2	'Which do you want, **this** one or **that** one?' – The assistant asked Neil if he wanted **the blue sweater** or **the yellow one**.	**Demonstrativpronomina:** Manches, was in der wörtlichen Rede offensichtlich ist, muss beim Berichten **näher erklärt** werden, z. B. wer spricht mit wem (§ 6.1) oder worauf beziehen sich Wörter wie *this, it* usw.
§ 6.3	Joe: 'I can't come **tonight**.' – Joe said he can't come **tonight**. (gleicher Zeitbezug) – Joe phoned this morning. He said he couldn't come **last night** because his car broke down. (anderer Zeitbezug) Mary: 'I'm going to New York **this summer**.' – Mary told me she is/was going to New York **this/that summer/ last year/in 2004**.	**Zeitangaben** werden wie folgt **geändert**, wenn der **Zeitbezug** der Berichtssituation **anders** ist als der der wörtlichen Rede. Wenn der Zeitbezug aber **noch zutrifft**, bleiben die Zeitangaben **unverändert**. – *now* — *at that time/then* – *today* — *that day/ last Sunday)/ on (May 2/Friday)* – *yesterday* — *the day before/ last …/ on (Tuesday)* – *tomorrow* — *the next day/ last …/on …*

zu § 6.3		– this week – that week – last month – the previous month/ the month before/ last …/in (May) – a few days – a few days before/ ago last …/on … – next year – the next year/ the following year/ in …
§ 6.4	Brian: 'I'm glad to be **here**.' – Brian said he was glad to be **back home/in Scotland/with his friends** … .	**Ortsangaben** werden nur dann **geändert**, wenn der **Ortsbezug** der wörtlichen Rede **nicht zutrifft**. Meistens muss eine **nähere Erklärung** gegeben werden.
§ 6.5	Mother: '**How much** did the CD cost?' – My mother **wanted to know how much** the CD cost. Diane: '**What shall** I do?' – Diane didn't know **what to do**.	**Fragen mit Fragewörtern** und mit *shall* werden als **indirekte Fragen** wiedergegeben.
§ 6.6	Ann: 'Do you watch TV much?' – Ann asked **if** I watch TV much. Ann: 'Do you prefer to read **or** watch TV?' – Ann asked **whether/(if)** I prefer/preferred to read or watch TV.	Für **Entscheidungsfragen** braucht man in der indirekten Rede *if/whether*. *If* klingt **informeller**. *Whether* steht oft **bei Entscheidungsfragen**. Häufige Verben: *ask, wonder, not know, want to know*.

12 Indirect speech — Übungen

8

Use the box to report what these people said or did.

1. Carol ... a boy ... .
2. Jeff offered to look after ... cat while she is on holiday.
3. Tom told me that Barbara is starting her new job ... .
4. I met Alan in town last week. He said that he had met a fantastic girl ... and that he was taking her out ... .
5. Linda invited Joe to her party ... .
6. Kevin ... we are going with him.

- the next day
- wanted to know
- last week
- standing near the window
- if
- on Monday
- the night before
- pointed to
- Mrs Smith's

Lösungen

1 Simple present – present progressive

Test 1
a) Margaret ist in Sheffield zu Hause.
b) Margaret wohnt zur Zeit in Sheffield.

Test 2

1. don't drink (§ 1.2)
2. are … learning – want (§ 2.2; § 3.3)
3. do … come (§ 1.3)
4. does … do (§ 1.1)
5. is training (§ 2.2)
6. tells (§ 1.4)
7. are … reading (§ 2.1/§ 2.2)
8. do … get (§ 1.6)
9. talks (§ 1.2)
10. are … doing (§ 2.1/2.5)
11. are … getting on (§ 2.3)
12. do … speak (§ 1.3)
13. is getting (§ 2.4)
14. is … asking (§ 2.5)

Übungen (S. 12–15)

1

Can you find the right pairs?
1–b; 2–e; 3–a; 4–f; 5–d; 6–c

2

She is sitting in an armchair.
She is wearing a pullover and trousers.
She is reading.
She is having a drink.
She is making a cupboard.
She drives a car.
She reads newspapers.
She listens to music.

She reads books/thrillers/murder stories.
She drinks tea.
She is listening to music.
She plays tennis.
She does not smoke.
She has a cat.
She is learning Spanish.

3

1. Do … want (§ 3.3)
2. are … telling (§ 2.5)
3. is dying (§ 2.4)
4. do … let (§ 1.2)
5. hear (§ 3.4)
6. says (§ 1.4)
7. looks (§ 3.1 a)
8. am travelling (§ 2.3)
9. does … get (§ 1.1)
10. sounds (§ 3.1 a)
11. am slimming (§ 2.3)
12. comes (§ 1.3)
13. tries … finds … belongs
    (tries, finds – § 1.7;
    belongs – § 3.1 b)
14. do … do? (§ 1.6);
    put … take (§ 1.5/§ 1.6)
15. Does … belong (§ 3.1b)

2 Simple past – present perfect

Test

1. bought (§ 1)
2. has had (§ 2.1)
3. went (§ 1)
4. have just been (§ 2.2)
5. have not done (§ 2.4)
6. did (§ 1)
7. did not sleep (§ 1)
8. have had (§ 2.3)
9. has been (§ 2.5)
10. have lost (§ 2.3); Did you take (§ 1)
11. did you go (§ 1)
12. have you been (§ 2.3)
13. Have you ever had (§ 2.4); broke (§ 1)
14. have you known (§ 2.1); started (§ 1)
15. has started (§ 2.1)

Übungen (S. 21–23)

1

§ 2.3

2

1. Der Zustand dauert noch an: ich gehe noch in diese Schule.
2. Der Zustand dauert nicht mehr an: Ich gehe nicht mehr in diese Schule.
3. 'This morning' ist noch nicht vorbei.
4. 'This morning' ist schon vorbei.

In Sätzen 5, 8, 9 und 12 deuten die *simple past* Formen darauf hin, dass der Sprecher an einen bestimmten Zeitpunkt denkt. Dieser Zeitbezug wird in Satz 12 durch die zusätzliche Information *a few weeks ago* deutlich.

Gebrauch des *present perfect*:
Sätze 1, 3 – § 2.1   –   Sätze 6, 7 – § 2.4   –   Sätze 10, 11 – § 2.3

3

We haven't had ... today zeigt, dass *today* noch nicht vorbei ist (§ 2.1); *You forgot* bezieht sich auf eine bestimmte Zeit vor dem Zeitpunkt des Sprechens, auch wenn diese nicht explizit erwähnt wird, nämlich *when you arrived this morning* (§ 1).

4

Where did you find your key?
I have finished my homework now.
I have written four letters since two o'clock.
Did you go on holiday last year?
My parents have never been abroad.
How long have you lived here now?
Why didn't you like the film?
Has your penfriend answered your letter yet?
I have just heard the news.
My mother lent me her car last night.

5

Carol: were
have just left
Have you applied
Who told you
did you talk to
asked – wanted – did you tell her?
Have you ever been

Mark: happened?
Did you get up late?
didn't have
have had – left – Didn't you like
Did you learn
have you ever visited

Present perfect:
have just left
Have you applied ... yet
Have you ever been
have had ... since (up to now)
Have you ever visited

3 Past progressive – simple past

Test
1. was getting, got (§ 2.1)
2. was wearing, arrived (§ 2.1)
3. was thinking (§ 1.2b)
4. were still enjoying (§ 1.1)
5. enjoyed (im Gegensatz zu § 1.1)
6. rang, was having (§ 2.1)
7. was going (§ 1.2a)
8. did not hear, was listening (§ 2.1)
9. was talking, was thinking (§ 2.2)
10. was wondering (§ 1.2c)
11. could not stop, was catching (§ 1.4)
12. stopped, caught (§ 2.2)
13. was driving, happened (§ 2.1)
14. got, finished, grabbed, ran (§ 2.2)
15. was coming (§ 1.3)

Übungen (S. 28–31)

1
were giving, were all wearing, was having, was playing, were dancing, werestanding, talking, laughing, was eating, drinking
screamed
arrived, interviewed
Inspector: were you doing
Miss G.: was talking
General: were telling
Inspector: were you doing
Mr Steel: was dancing

2
1. a) When I got to the party everyone went home.
   b) When I got to the party everyone was going home.
2. a) What were you doing when the lights went out? I was having a shower.
   b) What did you do when the lights went out? I lit a candle.
3. a) The girl was drowning, but they saved her.
   b) The girl drowned. They couldn't save her.

4. a) When the phone rang I got out of the shower and answered it.
   b) When the phone rang I was having a shower, so I couldn't answer it.
5. a) When I looked at the baby it was crying.
   b) When I looked at the baby it cried.
6. a) What did you do when your brother fell into the river? I jumped in after him.
   b) What were you doing when your brother fell into the river? I was just a few metres away, fishing.

Differences:
1. Als ich ankam,
   a) machten sich alle auf den Weg nach Hause.
   b) waren alle schon am Weggehen.
2. a) Als die Lichter ausgingen, war ich gerade unter der Dusche.
   b) Die Lichter gingen aus, daraufhin zündete ich eine Kerze an.
3. a) Das Mädchen war am Ertrinken, aber es wurde gerettet.
   b) Das Mädchen ist ertrunken. Es konnte nicht gerettet werden.
4. Als das Telefon klingelte,
   a) stieg ich aus der Badewanne und meldete mich.
   b) war ich in der Badewanne, konnte mich also nicht melden.
5. a) Das Baby hat schon, bevor ich es ansah, geweint.
   b) Das Baby weinte, weil ich es ansah.
6. Als mein Bruder in den Fluss fiel,
   a) bin ich ihm nachgesprungen.
   b) habe ich ein paar Meter weiter weg geangelt.

3

1. were still waiting
2. arrived, was just leaving
3. was planning
4. were you talking to, saw
5. were not able to visit, was being repaired
6. were doing
7. were thinking
8. Did you see, was wearing
9. started, was watching, put
10. were going
11. heard, locked, ran, fetched
12. was staying, met
13. was wondering

4
1. a) When the teacher walked in the pupils were listening to music and dancing.
   b) When the teacher walked in the pupils stopped dancing.
2. a) Linda went home by taxi because she missed the last bus.
   b) John went home by taxi because it was raining so hard.
3. a) I did not hear the announcement because somebody was talking.
   b) I did not hear the announcement because somebody switched the radio off.

5
One day Santa Claus could not find his reindeers. So he went out to look for them. It was snowing. Suddenly he met two men. They were sitting next to a fire. On the fire (there) was a saucepan with food in it. The men were eating some meat. The meat looked like Santa's reindeers. When Santa saw what the men were eating he (started to cry/was very angry/hit one of them/went to get a policeman/asked if he could have some, too/ate some, too …).

4 Present perfect progressive – present perfect simple – past perfect

Test 1
1. have done (§ 2.1, § 4)
2. have been doing (§ 1.1, § 2.3, § 4)
3. have you been doing; have been reading … haven't finished (§ 1.2, § 1.2, § 2.1)
4. has been making … has made (§ 1.1, § 2.2, § 4)
5. has … been going (§ 1.1, § 4)
6. have … known (§ 1.2b)
7. has been trying (§ 1.2, § 2.3, § 4)
8. has tried (§ 2.2, § 4)
9. have … liked (§ 1.2b)

Test 2
1. It has been raining all day. (§ 1.1, § 2.3)
2. How long have you been waiting for me? (§ 1.1)
3. I have known my girlfriend for three months. (§ 1.2b)
4. Julie has been painting all day. (§ 1.1, § 2.3)
5. How long have you been learning English? You're very good. (§ 1.1, § 2.3)
6. Your eyes are red. Have you been crying? (§ 1.2, § 2.2)
7. I'm tired. I've been working very hard today. (§ 1.2, § 2.2)
8. Sally has had a cold for ages. (§ 1.2b)
9. We have been living here for two years. (§ 1.1)

Übungen (S. 35–43)

1

1. It is raining.
2. It has been raining since this morning.
3. Mr Williams has been talking for an hour.
4. Mr Williams is talking about his operation.
5. My girlfriend is learning Italian.
6. My girlfriend has been learning Italian for six months.

'For' und 'since' sind Signalwörter für das 'present perfect continuous'.

2

1. Dad has been making dinner since (ten o'clock, he got up …)/for (two hours …).
2. Grandad has been singing since (breakfast, he came home …)/for (half an hour …).
3. My boyfriend has been working on his computer since (he came home from school, five o'clock …)/for (three hours …).
4. Kevin has been looking for a job since (March …)/for (three months …).

3

1. He has been driving for six months. (§ 2.3)
   He has driven about five thousand kilometres. (§ 2.1)
2. 'Yes, I have been slimming.' (§ 2.2)
   'Yes, I have lost a lot of weight.' (§ 2.1)
3. 'Yes, I have been explaining something to him.' (§ 1.2)
   'Oh, I have explained it so often, but he still can't do it.' (§ 2.1)

4

1. How long have you been waiting?
2. How long have you been collecting stamps?
   How many have you collected?
3. How long has he been on holiday?
4. How long have you been smoking?
   How many have you smoked today?
5. How long have you had a/that cold?
6. How often have I told you to ask me before you borrow anything?

How long ist ein Signalwort für das *present perfect progressive*.
Ausnahmen: Verben, wie *be* (Frage 3), *have* (Frage 5), *like, love, see, hear, know, remember, wish, belong, …*) die normalerweise keine *progressive form* bilden. (Vgl. § 1.2b).

5

1. I have had six cups of tea already. And your mother has just poured me a seventh.
2. I have been drinking tea all day. There was nothing else to do.
3. Charlie has drunk eight pints of beer. I could never drink so many.
4. Charlie has been drinking. Now he can't stand up.
5. I have been walking to school all week. The buses were on strike.
6. I have often walked to school. Haven't you?
7. Dennis has been spending a lot of money lately. I wonder where he got it from?
8. Dennis has spent a lot of money on his motor bike. Have you seen it?

6

1. How long has she been learning judo?
   When did she start learning judo?
2. How long has she been waiting?
   When did she arrive?
3. How long has he been working there?
   When did he leave Wales?

7

Mrs Gambol: How did you do it?
Mr Gambol: I have been using my pocket calculator all day.

8

It's 10.30. Mike <u>has done</u> some washing. He <u>started</u> at 10.00 and he <u>has been doing</u> it <u>for</u> half an hour.
It's 11.10. Mike <u>has made</u> a cake and he <u>has started</u> to <u>paint</u> a cupboard. He <u>has been painting</u> it since 11.00.
It's 12.15. Mike <u>started</u> to <u>practise</u> half an hour ago. He has <u>been practising since</u> 11.45.
It's 14.00. Mike <u>has had</u> his lunch. After that he <u>washed</u> the pots. He <u>has been writing</u> letters <u>for</u> half an hour.
It's 14.45. Mike has <u>been playing table tennis since</u> 14.00.
It's 16.30. Mike <u>has put</u> his holiday photos into an album. Now he <u>is doing</u> the ironing. He <u>has been doing it/has been ironing for</u> half an hour.
Now it's 19.00. Mike <u>has had</u> his tea and <u>has fallen</u> asleep. He <u>has been</u> asleep <u>since</u> 18.00.

5 Future time

Test
1. am playing (§ 4)
2. does … end? (§ 5.1)
3. aren't (§ 5.2)
4. is going to (§ 3.2)
5. will be (§ 2.1)
6. 'll (§ 2.3)
7. leave (§ 5.2) (if, when)
8. is going to (§ 3.1)
9. will be doing (§ 6.1)
10. will have finished (§ 7.1)
11. will have been working (§ 7.2)

Übungen (S. 49–57)

1
1. a) I'll get some.
   b) I'm going to get some envelopes.
2. I'll – spontane Äußerung: I'm going to – fester Entschluss
3. I'll – spontane Äußerung
4. I'm going to – fester Entschluss
5. I'm going to – fester Entschluss
6. I'll – spontane Äußerung

2
1. is going to (§ 3.2)
2. will (§ 2.2), after 'think';
   am going to (§ 3.1)
3. 'll (§ 2.3)
4. will (§ 2.1)
5. are you going to (§ 3.1);
   will (§ 2.2), after 'expect'
6. going to (§ 3.2)
7. 'll (§ 2.3)
8. will (§ 2.2), after 'sure'
9. are you going to (§ 3.1)
10. won't (§ 2.1)

3

1. It is raining/going to rain tomorrow.
   It is raining tomorrow bedeutet, dass es aufgrund eines vereinbarten Planes regnen wird, was nicht möglich ist.
2. You're falling/going to fall if you're not careful.
   You're falling bedeutet, dass die Person aufgrund eines vereinbarten Planes fallen wird, was hier sinnlos ist.

4

Satz 1 ist die bessere Ausrede. Das *present progressive* drückt aus, dass der Plan fest ist und nicht verändert werden kann. Satz 2 drückt aus, dass man zwar etwas vor hat, dass der Plan aber noch nicht so fest ist wie in Satz 1.

5

1. eat … will get   2. drive … will not have   3. will see … go   4. order … will be

6

1. If   2. if   3. when   4. when   5. If   6. when

7

if; (§ 3.1)

8

1. starts
2. is having
3. are going …
   Are you coming
4. is your friend coming
5. does the bus leave

9

1. will be learning
2. will be playing
3. will still be working

Rule (§ 6.1)

10

"Will you be driving back?" Klingt nicht so aufdringlich.
1. Will you be using …
2. Will you be passing the post office?
3. I'll be seeing him this afternoon.
4. No problem. I'll be going shopping soon.

11
1. I'll fly – spontaner Entschluss (§ 2.3)
2. I am going to fly – fester Vorsatz (§ 3.1)
3. I am flying – fest beschlossener Plan (§ 4)
4. I fly – Teil eines festgelegten Programms (§ 5.1)
5. I'll be flying – ich fahre immer im Sommer, sowieso (§ 6.2)

12
They will have cleaned the room/decorated it/mended the window/painted the walls, cupboard/put a carpet on the floor/brought some more furniture/put some posters up (put some posters on the walls)/put some curtains up.

13
1. is helping (§ 4)
2. will pass (§ 2.2), nach 'sure'
3. is playing (§ 4)
4. will get (§ 2.1)
5. do … close (§ 5.1)
6. 'll lend (§ 2.3)
7. don't (§ 5.2)
8. are … staying (§ 4)
9. will have finished (§ 7.1)
10. will be working (§ 6.1)
11. leaves (§ 5.1)
12. is (§ 5.2)
13. won't be living (§ 6.1)
14. will have gone (§ 7.1)
15. doesn't come (§ 5.2)
16. does … arrive (§ 5.1)

6 Modals

Test 1
1. can't have gone (§ 1.10)
2. must still be (§ 2.3)
3. must have gone (§ 3)
4. must be going (§ 2.3)
5. might have gone (§ 6.6)
6. might be playing (§ 6.5)
7. shouldn't have stayed up (§ 7.7)
8. should be doing (§ 7.5)
9. will be able to speak (§ 1.12)
10. could have gone (§ 1.9)

Test 2
1. 'Would you like/Do you want to go swimming?' (§ 9.3)
   'No, I don't want to just now.'
2. Shall I bring you a newspaper? (§ 7.1)
3. 'I have to get up at seven every day.' (§ 4.1)
   'I don't have/need to get up so early.' (§ 4.3; § 5.1)
4. I'm afraid I couldn't ring yesterday. I had to go out. (§ 1.5; § 4.1)
5. Our friends should/are supposed to arrive tomorrow. (§ 7.3; § 7.8)
6. Our friends should have arrived/were supposed to arrive yesterday. (§ 7.7)
7. I'll try to repair your old cassette recorder. It shouldn't be too difficult. (§ 7.3)
8. You don't have/need to go shopping. I've brought everything (with me). (§ 4.3; § 5.1)
9. You mustn't go shopping with that cold. (§ 5.2)
10. You shouldn't go shopping with that cold. (§ 7.2)

Übungen (S. 62–81)

1
1. We could have it next Saturday.
2. You could give her a book.
3. We could have some hamburgers.

2
1. Could I borrow your umbrella, please?
2. Could you help me with my homework, please?
3. Could I ask you something, please?

3
1. Will I be able to speak French next year? (§ 1.12)
2. You can come if you bring a/some girl(s) with you. (§ 1.2)
3. I think I'll be able to buy it next year. (§ 1.12)

4
1. He was not able to play.
2. He was not allowed to play.
3. a) Is it possible for you to come on holiday with us?
   b) Are you allowed to come …

5
1. Can you speak French? (§ 1.1)
2. I could speak French quite well ten years ago. (§ 1.5)
3. You could/would be able to find a better job if you learned a foreign language. (§ 1.6)
4. Could I borrow your bike, please? (§ 1.7)
5. Can you lend me your bike? (§ 1.2)
6. I can't/am not allowed to go to the cinema. (§ 1.2)
7. I can't go to the cinema, I've got too much homework. (§ 1.3)
8. Maria will soon be able to ski if she practises a bit. (§ 1.11)
9. I could run very fast when I was a child. (§ 1.5)
10. I've never been able to play table-tennis. (§ 1.12)
11. Can I carry/take your bag? (§ 1.4)
12. That can't be the right answer. (§ 1.10)

6
It doesn't matter what I wear. Your son must wear school uniform.

7
You must keep off the grass. You mustn't walk on the grass.
You must put your litter in the basket. You mustn't throw it on the ground.
Tony must remember to feed the hamster. Tony mustn't forget to feed the hamster.
You mustn't take any food into the library/mustn't eat/drink in the library.
You must drive 30 or less. You mustn't go faster than 30.

8

a) der Sprecher ist sich dessen sicher.
b) der Sprecher ist sich nicht so sicher. Aufgrund von bestimmten Merkmalen wird eine Schlussfolgerung gezogen, die wahrscheinlich stimmt.
1. Kay must know a lot of people.
2. Bill can't earn very much.
3. You can't be tired already.
4. It must be the postman.

9

1. must be learning French
2. must have gone away
3. can't have thrown it away
4. must be joking
5. can have heard you
6. must have forgotten to switch it off

10

1. had to   2. has had to   3. mustn't   4. Did … have to   5. did … have to   6. Does … have to   7. does … have to – has to   8. don't have to   9. must (have to)   10. do … have to …? Do … have to   11. have to   12. must (have to)

11

1. a) Das stört mich.
   b) Das brauchst du nicht.
   a) I don't like it.
   b) I can hear you/I'm not deaf.

2. a) Du darfst es ihm nicht sagen.
   b) Du brauchst es ihm nicht zu sagen.
   a) It's a secret/I don't want him to know.
   b) But you can if you want/He knows already.

12

1. mustn't   2. needn't/don't have to   3. needn't/don't have to … mustn't

13

1. a)   2. b)

14
1. 'I needn't have sold my stamps.'
2. 'I needn't have taken my umbrella.'
3. '… I didn't need to pay.'

15
1. I can leave school next year.
2. I may/might leave school next year.
3. Cigarettes may/might damage your health.
4. Cigarettes can damage your health.

16
1. She might not be coming today.
2. She might be ill.
3. She might have gone to the doctor's.
4. She might not have heard the alarm.
5. She might have been dancing all night.

17
a) Mike must have told her.
b) Mike might have told her.
c) Mike can't have told her.

18
You should go jogging.
You shouldn't smoke.
You must turn left/mustn't turn right.
You mustn't smoke.
… we use <u>should</u>.

19
1. 'This maths homework is very difficult.' 'Shall I help you?'
2. My little sister should have been home an hour ago. Do you think we should phone the police?
3. 'I know a very poor family.' 'You ought to give them some money.'
4. I suppose I should do my homework, but I don't want to.
5. 'What's Ken's phone number?' 'How should I know?'
6. This film should interest you. It's about Great Britain.
7. People should/ought to drive more slowly.
8. You'd better not break that cup.

20
"I suppose we shouldn't have (eaten them) really."

21
1. I'll
2. won't
3. Will
4. Would
5. wouldn't
6. Will … don't want to/won't
7. won't
8. won't

22
I'd certainly like it again tomorrow.
I'd like it again and again.
… you might get it right.

7 Infinitive – ing-Form

Test 1
1. reading (§ 3.1), to borrow (§ 1.1)
2. not to work (§ 1.2a), take (§ 2.2)
3. going (§ 3.3), watching (§ 3.3)
4. watching (§ 3.3)
5. not to go (§ 1.1a)
6. go (§ 2.1)
7. looking (§ 3.2), finding (§ 3.2)
8. spilling (§ 3.2)
9. stay (§ 2.2), go (§ 2.2)
10. to have been (§ 1.1a)
11. being bitten (§ 3.2)
12. cutting (§ 3.4), being told (§ 3.1)
13. buy (§ 2.1)

Test 2
1. Have you decided <u>what to do</u> yet? (§ 1.1d)
2. Have you (got) <u>anyone to talk to</u>? (§ 1.1c)
3. If you <u>want me to help</u> you you will have to wait a little/a bit. (§ 1.2b)
4. 'Shall we have a cup of tea?' 'I'd love <u>to</u>.' (§ 1.6 Beachte:)
5. We waited <u>to see</u> what would happen. (§ 1.6)

Test 3
1. a) Tanzst du gern (normalerweise)?
   b) Möchtest du jetzt tanzen? (§ 1.2b)
2. a) Sich an etwas in der Vergangenheit erinnern: ing-Form (§ 4.2a)
   b) Sich erinnern, etwas zu tun: Infinitiv (§ 4.2a)
3. a) Aufhören, etwas zu tun: ing-Form (§ 4.2b)
   b) Aufhören, um etwas zu tun: Infinitiv (§ 4.2b)
4. a) Man sieht den ganzen Vorgang, vom Anfang bis zum Schluss: Infinitiv (§ 4.3)
   b) Man sieht nur den Teil des Vorgangs, der sich gerade im Ablauf befindet: ing-Form (§ 4.3)

Übungen (S. 86–95)

1
1. Would you like to dance with me? (§ 1.2b)
2. I asked Mike to dance (with me), but he refused/didn't want to. (§ 1.2a; 1.6 Beachte:) I wish I had never asked him. (§ 1.4)
3. My penfriend has invited me to stay with her in the holidays. (§ 1.2a)
4. Will your parents pay for you to go to England on holiday? (§ 1.5)
5. The teacher advised Thomas to go to (Great) Britain to improve his English. (§ 1.2a, 1.6)
6. Is it easy for foreigners to get holiday jobs in Britain? (§ 1.5)
7. I'm looking for someone to help me to find a holiday job. I don't know who to ask. (§ 1.1c, 1d)
8. It's difficult for me to explain what I want to say/what I mean/to express myself in English. (§ 1.5)
9. 'Do you know how to fill this form in?' 'No, and there's no-one to ask.' (§ 1.1d, 1c)
10. Can you wait for me to change money? (§ 1.5)
11. Susan wished (that) she had not invited John to her party. (§ 1.4)
12. Do you want me to come early? (§ 1.2b)
13. 'Does your sister want to come (with us)?' 'She'd like to, but I don't want her to. (§ 1.1a, 1.6 Beachte:)

2
Viele Sätze sind möglich, nur müssen Sie aufpassen, dass auf *make* und *let* ein Infinitiv ohne *to* folgt, z. B. *Our teachers let us wear what we like.* Auf *allow* und *have to* folgt dagegen immer *to*: *Our teachers allow us to wear what we like.*

3
1. b) I don't want to lend you my camera.
2. a) We have arranged to meet at the town hall.
   b) Why not meet at the bus stop instead?
3. a) We had better get some more bread.
   b) John asked Eric to get some more bread.
4. a) Would you rather stay in or go out?
   b) I've decided to stay in.

4
1. I'm <u>looking forward to lying</u> on the beach.
2. Thomas was <u>not used to drinking</u> tea with milk.
3. Do you <u>feel like listening</u> to a record?
4. Would you <u>mind taking</u> me to town, please?
5. Neil <u>can't stand being</u> alone.
6. Carol <u>enjoys being</u> alone.

5
The cat <u>kept playing</u> with the wool. Rule § 3.1

6
1. to meet
2. meeting … bring
3. mending … to do
4. working … to do … seeing
5. cry
6. crying
7. to explain
8. making
9. to use
10. being criticised
11. waiting … getting
12. smoking … not to smoke
13. worrying … forget
14. going … get … leave
15. leaving … to work
a) Regel § 3.1 – 6, 10, 12 (give up)
b) Regel § 3.2 – 2 (look forward to), 4 (tired of), 8, 14 (fed up with), 15 (after)
c) Regel § 3.3 – 4 (What about …?), 11 (no point in, it's not worth), 13 (it's no good)
d) Regel § 3.4 – 3

7
§ 3.2

8
He has remembered to collect the coat, buy the newspapers, buy Jane's birthday present.
He has forgotten to take the library books back, water the flowers, post the letters, empty the rubbish bin.
I must remember to/mustn't forget to take the library books back, water the flowers, post the letters, empty the rubbish bin.

9
Do you remember <u>going</u> into hospital when you were ten; <u>wanting</u> to be a doctor?
I'll never forget <u>learning</u> to ride a bike; <u>going</u> out with a girl/boy for the first time.
I'll always remember <u>crying</u> on my first day at school; <u>earning</u> my first money.

10
1. to do … asking
2. having
3. to save up
4. putting
5. talking
6. to talk
7. to have
8. singing

11
1. play
2. playing
3. singing
4. play
5. playing
6. come
7. turn
8. sitting
9. sit

§ 4.3

12
'I hope we're in time to see them being fed.'

8 Participles

Test
1. Als es an der Haustüre klingelte, rannte Ann nach unten. (§ 1.1.3)
2. Jill schnitt sich in den Finger, als sie ihr Fahrrad reparierte. (§ 1.1.2)
3. Kannst du mich bitte dem Mädchen am Fenster vorstellen. (§ 1.2.6)
4. Vier Jungen saßen auf dem Boden und spielten Karten. (§ 1.1.1)
5. Nachdem man uns Marias neue Wohnung vorgeführt hatte, fanden wir sie alle sehr schön. (§ 1.1.3)
6. Willst du die Wohnung tapezieren lassen, oder willst du es selber machen? (§ 2.3)
7. Kevin stand völlig fasziniert vor dem Gemälde. (§ 2.1; § 1.2.2)
8. Glaubst du nicht, dass Diane besser aussieht, wenn ihre Haare lose herunterhängen? (§ 1.2.3)
9. Ich habe meinen Schirm im Flur stehen lassen. (§ 2.2)
10. Nach einer schlaflosen Nacht waren wir alle sehr müde. (§ 1.2.1)
11. Obwohl er wenig bezahlt bekommt, hat Eric seine neue Arbeit gern. (§ 1.2.4)
12. Da sie arbeitslos ist, hat Jenny wenig Geld. (§ 1.2.1)
13. Wenn man bedenkt, dass die Preise täglich steigen, wundere ich mich, dass sich die Leute immer noch Autos leisten können. (§ 1.2.3)
14. Cathy war so über das Interview am nächsten Tag beunruhigt, dass sie nicht schlafen konnte. (§ 1.2.1)
15. Es ist verboten, ohne zwingenden Grund auf der Autobahn zu halten. (§ 1.2.5)
16. Wie wäre es mit einem kostenlosen Wochenende in einem Luxushotel? (§ 1.2.3)

Übungen (S. 101–105)

1
1. Alan was lying on his bed listening to the radio.
2. Jeff broke his leg skiing.
3. Hearing the phone ring, Sue got up to answer it.
4. I got home feeling tired.
5. Walking past the shop, I remembered I needed some milk.

Satz 3: § 1.1.3
Satz 2: § 1.1.2
Bei den anderen Sätzen: § 1.1.1

2
When/While I was …

3

1. (which was)   2. (who is)   3. (who were)   4. (which are)

4

a Mexican riding a bike; a bear climbing a tree; a giraffe walking past a window (Rule § 1.2.6)

5

1. with you interrupting me
2. with travel becoming cheaper
3. with only a few more minutes left
4. with buses running every ten minutes

6

1. Da sie seit zwei Jahren in Amerika arbeitet, hat meine Schwester sehr viele Freunde dort.
2. Als er ein Geräusch hörte, wachte Tony auf.
3. Sue rannte aus dem Haus und schlug die Türe hinter sich zu.
4. Ich konnte meinen Bruder gestern nicht alleine lassen, da er sich nicht wohl fühlte.
5. Riechst du, dass etwas brennt?
6. Geputzt und gestrichen würde das Fahrrad so gut wie neu aussehen.
7. Der Hund rannte uns entgegen.
8. Als Ausländer brauchen Sie/braucht man ein Visum, um in diesem Land zu bleiben.
9. Als man sie fragte, wie sie die Prüfung fand, sagte Maria, dass sie zu einfach war.
10. Obwohl sie überrascht war, sagte Carol nichts.
11. Alan legte enttäuscht den Hörer auf, weil Dave nicht kommen konnte.
12. Diese Dose explodiert, wenn man sie an einem warmen Ort stehen lässt.
13. Der See sieht schön aus, wenn die Sonne darauf scheint.

7

- You always keep me <u>waiting</u>.
- You always leave the radio <u>switched on</u>, ...
- You keep <u>reading</u> my library books.
- ... catch you <u>using</u> my comb again.
- You sit <u>doing</u> nothing ... standing <u>selling</u> records
- ... get your hair <u>cut</u>

8

1. weather permitting   2. Seeing that   3. generally speaking   4. Supposing   5. judging from

9 If-clauses

Test 1
1. If I have time I'll help you. (§ 1)
2. When I have time I'll help you. (§ 1)
3. If I miss the bus I'll take a taxi. (§ 2.1)
4. I won't go/am not going to your friends'/to see your friends unless they invite me/I am invited. (§ 2.2)
5. I won't go/am not going even if I am invited. (§ 2.2)
6. My father talks to me as if I were a child. (§ 4.2)

Test 2
Man ist eher sicher: 1,3 (§ 2.1)
Man ist sich nicht so sicher: 2,4 (§ 4.1)

Test 3
1. give (§ 1)
2. gave (§ 4.3)
3. sells (§ 1)
4. sold (§ 4.1)
5. had sold (§ 5.1)
6. would … take (§ 4.1)
7. would … have taken (§ 5.1)
8. were (§ 4.2)
9. had (§ 4.2)
10. gets (§ 1)
11. had not broken down (§ 5.1)
12. didn't wear (§ 4.3)
13. went (§ 4.3)
14. had gone (§ 5.1)
15. might have passed (§ 5.1)
16. had not come (§ 5.1)
17. could speak (§ 4.1)

Übungen (S. 108–119)

1
1. a) <u>When</u> I go to town I'll bring you a magazine.
   b) <u>If</u> I go to town I'll bring you a magazine.
2. <u>Whenever</u> I go to town I (always) bring my mother a magazine (back).
3. <u>When</u> I am older I want to be a pop star.
4. We're not sure/don't know <u>if</u> we're going to Ireland. But <u>if</u> we do/<u>if</u> we go we'll stay/it will be for three weeks.
5. <u>Whenever</u> we go to Ireland we (always) visit/go and see my penfriend.
6. 'Did I leave my key at your place <u>when</u> I called (in) this morning?' 'I don't think so, but if I find it I'll ring/call you.'
7. <u>Whenever</u> I see pictures of New York I want to go there.
8. What would you do <u>if</u> you were bitten by a dog?
9. 'What shall we do <u>if</u> we miss the train?'

2

If you <u>want</u> to read this book I'll lend it to you.
If you <u>see</u> Sally tonight ask her to give me a ring.
If you <u>don't give up</u> smoking you'll be ill.
If you <u>play</u> in our team we should win.
If you <u>come</u> home early we can watch the match on TV.
If you <u>fill in</u> this form/fill this form <u>in</u> you can join the library.
If you <u>have</u> some free time come and see me.
If you <u>cross</u> a road in Britain look to the right first.

3

1. drives
2. is … talking
3. doesn't come
4. don't ask
5. haven't bought
6. don't like
7. is listening
8. hasn't got up … should be

4

1. if
2. unless
3. Even if
4. if
5. unless
6. even if

5

want … when … am

6

1b, 2a, 3a
1a, 2b, 3b

7

If Joe passes the exam his teachers will be very surprised.
If Joe passed the exam his teachers would be very surprised.
If the bank closes at three we won't be able to change money.
If the bank closed at three we wouldn't be able to change money.
If Harry gives Ann a lift she won't be late.
If Harry gave Ann a lift she wouldn't be late.
If the weather is fine we can have a picnic.
If the weather were fine we could have a picnic.

8

1. 'I'd come if I didn't have to work.'
2. 'I'd buy it if it weren't so expensive.'
3. 'I'd take it/the job if you paid me more.'
   'If they gave me more (money) I'd take it/the job.'
4. 'If only I weren't so fat.'
   'If you ate less cake you wouldn't be so fat.'
5. 'If you didn't go to bed so late all the time you wouldn't be (so) tired.'

9

1. 'How much would you have paid, then?'
2. 'What would you have said, then?'
3. 'Where would you have gone, then?'
4. 'When would you have gone, then?'

10

If Barbara hadn't gone outside with wet hair she wouldn't have caught cold.
If Frank hadn't lent Norman some money Norman couldn't have bought the bike.
If someone had told me Mr. Jones was ill I would have gone to see him.
If we hadn't brought a map we wouldn't know where to go now.
If Tony hadn't looked at a pretty girl he wouldn't have run into a lorry.
If Maria hadn't reminded Jeff about Ann's birthday he would have forgotten it.
If Sue had let Pete know she was coming he could/would have met her at the station.
If Caroline hadn't stayed up all night she wouldn't be tired today.
If Trevor hadn't lost his car keys we wouldn't have had to go by bus.
If the Marsdens hadn't told us about this hotel we wouldn't be staying here this week.
If Derek had worked hard(er) he would/might have passed the exam.

11
1. – b
2. – c
3. – a
4. – c

12
1. – c
2. – a
3. – b

13
1. were not/weren't
2. had not been/hadn't been
3. didn't take … were
4. had
5. had had
6. hadn't invited
7. don't invite
8. didn't invite
9. hadn't broken
10. would have played
11. learn
12. could drive

10 Comparison of adjectives

Test 1
a) taller, the tallest (§ 1.1a)
b) cleverer, the cleverest (§ 1.1b); ('more clever' gilt aber nicht mehr als falsch, vgl. § 1.1 Beachte:)
c) worse, the worst (§ 2)
d) more expensive, the most expensive (§ 1.2)
e) bigger, the biggest (§ 1.1a)
f) simpler, the simplest (§ 1.1b); ('more simple' wird auch akzeptiert, vgl. § 1.1 Beachte:)
g) better, the best (§ 2)
h) worse, the worst (§ 2)
i) shorter, the shortest (§ 1.1a)
j) more interesting, the most interesting (§ 1.2)
k) fatter, the fattest (§ 1.1 a)
l) more, the most (§ 2)
m) easier, the easiest (§ 1.1b); (auch 'more easy', vgl. § 1.1 Beachte:)
n) thinner, the thinnest (§ 1.1a)
o) more modern, the most modern (§ 1.2)
p) more, the most (§ 2)

Test 2
1. the most intelligent (§ 1.2)
2. more difficult than (§ 3.1)
3. faster than (§ 3.1)
4. as warm as (§ 3.2)
5. bigger (§ 1.1a)
6. more often (§ 1.2)
7. The more … the faster (§ 3.5)
8. better than … more romantic (§ 2; § 1.2)
9. harder and harder (§ 3.4)
10. the nicest (§ 1.1a)
11. More and more (§ 3.4)
12. as important as (§ 3.2)
13. The longer … the better (§ 3.5)

Übungen (S. 123–127)

1
lightest

2
1. earlier   2. older, happier   3. thinner   4. faster   5. better   6. more and more
7. more … cheaper

3
1. Most   2. worse   3. best   4. more   5. worst   6. most   7. least

4
1. taller than
   shorter than
2. as easy as
3. not as difficult as
   more difficult than
4. as useful as
5. not as hot as
   hotter than
6. bigger than
   not as big as
   more … than
   not as many … as
7. the highest
   higher than
   not as high as
8. the most expensive
   the cheapest
   more expensive than
9. Eleven thirty-two is earlier than twenty-seven minutes to twelve. Twenty-seven minutes to twelve is later than eleven thirty-two.

11 Adverbs

Test 1
1. awfully (§ 2.1)
2. critically (§ 2.1)
3. probably (§ 2.1)
4. in a friendly way (§ 2.2)
5. with difficulty (§ 1.3)
6. late (§ 2.3)
7. lately (§ 2.4)
8. hard … hardly (§ 2.4)
9. nice (§ 2.5)

Test 2
1. There is a train at ten to five tomorrow afternoon. (§ 3.3)
2. Do you still go to school? (§ 3.4c)
3. Sue hasn't found a job yet. (§ 3.5) She probably won't find one before Christmas either. (§ 7.2 Beachte:; § 8.4)
4. We went to the disco on Saturday. (§ 4.3b)
5. Mike speaks French quite well. (§ 7.1) Angela does, too. (§ 8.4)
6. Teresa always gets up early. (§ 6.2)
7. I went to the cinema three times last week. (§ 6.5b)
8. This shop only sells trousers. (§ 8.1)
9. 'I don't even know Karin's telephone number.' (§ 8.1) 'I don't either.' (§ 8.4)
10. I'm afraid I can't help you. I'm a stranger here, you see. However, I have a map of the town/city. Perhaps/Maybe it will help you. (§ 11)

Übungen (S. 133–147)

1
1. probably
2. Hopefully ('Hopefully' has now completely replaced 'I hope so' in spoken English.)
3. cheerful … happily
4. well
5. long
6. fantastically
7. weekly
8. absolutely
9. early … fast
10. in a friendly way

11. with difficulty
12. good … nice

2

1. Martin Luther King fought hard for the rights of black people.
2. Can you speak a bit louder, please? I can hardly hear you.
3. Helen lives near the station.
4. I nearly missed my bus yesterday.
5. This tower is very high.
6. This book is highly interesting.
7. I'll be late home this evening/tonight.
8. Have you seen Barbara lately?

(§ 2.4)

3

1. The shop doesn't close until eight on Fridays. (§ 3.3)
2. We should be home by about eleven. (§ 3.1)
3. I go out with my friends on Saturday nights. But on Sundays I go out with my parents. (§ 3.2)
3. We're going on holiday in August.
4. In September my penfriend is coming to see me. (§ 3.2)
5. The shop is still open. (§ 3.4b)
6. I still go to school. (§ 3.4a)
7. I haven't met my penfriend yet. (§ 3.5)
8. Do you still play the guitar? (§ 3.4c)

4

'That's the Empire State Building over there.'

5

1. My grandparents live in a little house in the country. (§ 4.3a)
2. I was born in a little village in the south in 1986./I was born in 1986 in a little village in the south. (§ 4.3a, b)
3. In Germany people drink a lot of coffee. In Britain they drink more tea. (§ 4.2)
4. We're going to France in July. (§ 4.3b)
5. The train arrives in Paris at seven forty-eight. (§ 4.3b)

6
1. He had lunch with Eve in town on Tuesday.
2. He watched a football match at Alan's on Wednesday afternoon.
3. He went to night school on Thursday evening.
4. He took Julie to the cinema on Friday evening.
5. He played table-tennis at the youth club on Saturday morning.

7
1. Your mother plays table-tennis surprisingly well.
2. Jennifer proudly showed us her stamp collection.
3. The sports teacher carefully explained the rules of the game.
4. Janet quickly put on her coat and rushed/ran out of the house.
5. Our neighbour angrily kicked our ball out of his garden.

Im Englischen darf das Adverb <u>nicht</u> zwischen <u>Verb</u> und <u>Objekt</u> stehen (§ 5 Beachte:).

8
1. I usually go to bed about ten o'clock.
2. I always get up rather early. etc.
   Rule § 6.

9
1. The Donalds have always lived in the country. (§ 6.2)
2. We have sports once a week. (§ 6.4)
3. Susan has never been to a pop concert. (§ 6.2)
4. Derek has been out with Linda a few times. (§ 6.4)
5. I always have to tell my parents where I'm going. (§ 6.2 Beachte:)
6. I can never remember that girl's name. (§ 6.2)

10
1. seriously ill
2. nearly missed
3. terribly sorry
4. very cheap
5. probably won't be able
6. completely changed
7. quite a nice … quite interesting
8. really know … probably be

11
1. I'm only going shopping/to the shops. I'll be back soon.
2. We only stayed at the concert for an hour. We couldn't even get seats.
3. Sue reads comics. But she also reads newspapers.
4. John can't come at the weekend. Mike can't (come) either.
5. 'I haven't done my homework yet.' 'I haven't either/Neither have I.'

12

1. <u>Unfortunately</u>, I can't meet you at the station./I can't meet you at the station, <u>unfortunately</u>.
2. <u>Surely</u> there's a bank (somewhere) around here./There's a bank (somewhere) around here, <u>surely</u>.
3. <u>Hopefully</u> I'll be able to go to England next summer./I'll be able to go England next summer, <u>hopefully</u>.
4. Whether I get the job depends, <u>of course</u>, on my exam results./<u>Of course</u>, whether …/Whether … results, <u>of course</u>.
5. <u>By the way</u>, have you seen Tony lately?/Have you seen Tony lately, <u>by the way</u>?
6. <u>Maybe/Perhaps</u> Sylvia is right.
7. <u>Basically</u> I agree with you./I agree with you, <u>basically</u>. There is, <u>however</u>, one difficulty./<u>However</u>, there is one difficulty.
8. <u>Luckily/Fortunately</u> the accident was not so bad.
9. "Shall we go to the football match?" "<u>Actually</u>, I don't like football. <u>In fact</u> I hate it."
"<u>Personally</u>, I'm not very interested in football either."

13

1. Hardly had we gone to bed when there was …
2. No sooner had Peter arrived than he had to …
3. Not only can Doreen play the piano, but she is also …

14

<u>No sooner had the children</u> arrived than they started running round the living-room.
<u>Not only did he</u> break the set, but also his leg …
<u>Hardly had the doctor</u> left when the little girl …
<u>Not only did she</u> break the window, she also cut …
<u>Not until</u> the children were in bed <u>could the Gambols</u> sit down and rest. "George," said Mrs Gambol, "<u>Under no circumstances are you</u> to invite those children again."

15

1. Don't keep laughing.
2. Andy seems to have a new job.
3. I used to like collecting stamps.
4. These days I prefer doing sports in my spare time.
5. Tony didn't pass the driving test, but he says he will go on trying.
He might/Maybe he'll be lucky the next time.
6. This fim is getting boring.
7. I'm afraid I can't come on Saturday.
8. Are you sure/certain that the train arrives at ten? – Yes, but it seems to be late.
9. Do you happen to have a map of London?
10. I think/suppose it's cheaper to go by train. I don't have much money, you see.

12 Indirect speech

Test
1. isn't (§ 2)
2. was doing (§ 3.1)
3. had known ... would have made (§ 3.1)
4. knew (§ 3.2)
5. a) wants (§ 3.4)
   b) wanted (§ 3.4)
6. likes/liked (§ 3.5)
7. didn't (§ 4.3)
8. a) had (§ 4.2)
   b) had/had had (§ 4.2)
9. a) can (§ 5.1)
   b) could (§ 5.1b)
10. a/the (§ 6.2)
11. the next day (§ 6.3)
12. what to do (§ 6.5)

Übungen (S. 151–164)

1
1. a) Mike <u>said</u> he would <u>help Steve</u>.
   b) Mike <u>promised</u> to help Steve.
2. Mr Reed <u>told Ben</u> to get <u>out of his garden</u>.
   b) Mr Reed <u>ordered/shouted to/warned</u> Ben to get <u>out of his garden</u>.
3. a) Frank <u>said (that) it</u> was cold.
   b) Frank <u>complained</u> that it was cold.
4. a) Mrs Williams <u>told her daughter</u> not to go <u>out without a coat</u>.
   b) Mrs Williams <u>warned/ordered/advised her daughter</u> not to go <u>out without a coat</u>.
5. a) <u>Mr Jennings said</u> that Sarah could <u>go to the pop concert</u>.
   b) Mr Jennings <u>finally allowed</u> Sarah to go <u>to the pop concert</u>.

2
1. Steve: 'I've <u>lost my passport</u>.'
   You to friend: Steve says he<u>'s lost his passport</u>.
2. Mary: 'My <u>money</u> has <u>been stolen</u>.'
   You to friend: Mary says her <u>money has been stolen</u>.
3. Martin: 'I'<u>m going to the cinema</u> tonight. Do you want <u>to go with me</u>?'
   You to friend: Martin says <u>he is going to the cinema</u> tonight. He asks if we <u>want to go with</u> him.
4. Derek: 'I <u>rang</u> you yesterday, but <u>you weren't in</u>. I'll <u>call in tonight</u>.'
   You to friend: Derek says <u>he rang</u> me yesterday, but <u>I wasn't in</u>. He says he<u>'ll call in tonight</u>.

3

1. had (§ 3.2)
2. was listening (§ 3.1a)
3. would (§ 3.1c); were (§ 3.2)
4. will (§ 3.4d)
5. would help (§ 3.1c)
6. could have helped … would have had … didn't want (§ 3.1b; § 3.1b; § 3.3)

4

1. (a). Bei (b) bekommt man den Eindruck, dass der Sprecher anderer Meinung ist. (§ 3.4)
2. (b); Urlaub steht noch bevor.
   (a); Urlaub ev. schon vorbei.
3. (a). Bei (b) könnte man den Eindruck bekommen, die Liebe ist schon vorbei. (§ 3.4)
4. (a). (§ 3.4)

5

1. a) is taking b) was taking
2. a) would be b) will be
3. a) saw b) had seen

6

1. a) should (§ 5.1a)
   b) should have (§ 5.1b)
2. might (§ 5.1b)
3. a) mustn't (§ 5.2b)
   b) should (§ 5.2b)

7

§ 5.1b

8

1. pointed to … standing near the window
2. Mrs Smith's
3. on Monday
4. the night before … the next day
5. last week
6. wanted to know … if

Abistoff – komplett und ausführlich

– Unverzichtbar für eine gründliche und intensive Vorbereitung in der Oberstufe
– Mit besonderen Extras für mehr Übersichtlichkeit:
  Zeitleisten, Versuchsdarstellungen und Formelsammlungen (je nach Fach)

 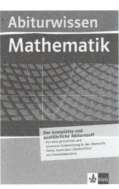 

Erhältlich im Buchhandel. www.klett.de/lernhilfen